Borderless Thalia

A Multilingual, Pandemic Comedic Collection

Edited by
Cătălina Florina Florescu

Solis Press

First published in 2022 by Solis Press, England

Compilation and foreword copyright © 2022
by Cătălina Florina Florescu.

Copyrights to individual plays and translations
remain with their authors.

Cover image: © Mircea G. Florescu, used with kind permission.

The authors of this work have asserted their rights under the Copyright, Design and Patents Act 1988 to be identified as the authors of this work.

All rights reserved. No part of this publication may be reproduced, stored in a retrieval system, or transmitted, in any form or by any means, electronic, mechanical, photocopying, recording or otherwise, except as permitted by the UK Copyright, Designs and Patents Act 1988, without the prior permission of the publisher.

This book is sold subject to the condition that it shall not, by way or trade or otherwise, be lent, resold, hired out or otherwise circulated without the publisher's prior consent in any form of binding or cover other than in which it is published and without a similar condition including this condition being imposed on the subsequent purchaser.

ISBN: 978-1-910146-80-4 (paperback)

ISBN: 978-1-910146-81-1 (hardback)

Ebooks are available

Published by Solis Press, Lytchett House, 13 Freeland Park,
Wareham Road, Poole BH16 6FA, England

Web: www.solispress.com | *Twitter*: @SolisPress

Contents

Foreword	iv
Christine Benvenuto You Are Muted *(English–Italian)*	1
Barbara Blatner Spell: A One-Act Riff in Verse on Shakespeare's *The Tempest* *(English–Romanian)*	11
Sarah Congress A Thanksgiving to Remember *(English–Spanish)*	26
Connie Dinkler Quarrel-tine *(English–Spanish)*	39
Selma Dragoș Tiny Frozen Doilies Falling from the Sky *(English–Romanian)*	48
Tjaša Ferme Two Lovers and a Bear: An Occult Romantic Comedy About Soul Mates and the Roles We Play *(English–Slovenian)*	66
Cătălina Florina Florescu Rehearsing Lines *(English–Greek)*	78
Avery Grace Cerebrum *(English–Spanish)*	86
Jinna Kim A Turkey Is Not a Rooster *(English–Korean)*	96
Elena Naskova Bottle Man: A Comedy *(English–Macedonian)*	101
Joyce Newman Scott The Bra Bust *(English–Portuguese)*	112
Ornella Ohayon What Comes After Sorrow *(English–French)*	120
Cindi Sansone-Braff To the Zoom and Back *(English–Spanish)*	134
Ellis Stump The People's Toast: A Contemporization of Václav Havel's Vaněk Plays *(English–Czech)*	142
Laurie Tanner Sex Ed for Mom *(English–Italian)*	158
Otilia Vieru-Baraboi Ana's Pictures: A Short Comedy on Nostalgia *(English–French)*	166
Biographies	183

Foreword

I used to tell my theater origin story by admitting how I had discovered theater on the radio, but I am actually wrong. I discovered theater in the simplest and purest ways possible, through role-playing.

I grew up in communist Romania and my older sister and I used to play together a lot. One of our activities was to line up our dolls and stuffed animals, and pretend they were on stage. We had this anthology of texts and one of them was from a play. While I can't remember its title or its author, I do know that while reciting the lines, the author would stop the "action" and instead employ this repetitive technique of literally saying the same lines over and over again. I would burst into laughter. I was fascinated by this repetition and, since I was playing, there was no pressure to be perfect. In retrospect, I realized how definitive that moment was for my becoming an educator, a playwright, and a friend. It is in repetition when we discover nuances that allow ourselves to be playful and enjoy the fluctuations of our voice, the changes in our physiognomy, and the *newness* of each repetitive act!

During the summer of 1989, I was fourteen years old and about to start high school. I had also returned from my first trip abroad to Denmark, and I was mesmerized by what I had seen and experienced. That same year, Romania would be communist-free. My language entered a new phase. Words such as "freedom," "protest," "rights," and "democracy" were entering my intimate vocabulary.

During the summer of 1990, my mother was telling me that she had breast cancer. I had to learn new words because of that too: "chemotherapy," "mastectomy," "morphine" and "intravenous therapy."

During the summer of 1998, I was graduating from University of Bucharest, ready to embark on a new journey, that of leaving my country of birth behind to earn my doctoral degree. Because of that decision, my vocabulary had yet to adapt itself and learn and live through words such as "mother tongue," "English as a second language," "citizenship," "borders," and "immigrant."

Cătălina Florina Florescu | FOREWORD

During the summer of 2020, I could not use my passport to travel back to Europe. At that time, there was no vaccine for COVID-19, and so I was looking at these new words while feeling everything magnified ten times, if not more: "trauma," "pandemic," "virus," "politics," and "survive."

All these four periods in my life are not only cardinal points in my professional development, but they have also changed my vocabulary and dramatic inclination to look at life and relationships with more care and devotion. All these four experiences – fall of communism, my mother's diagnosis and premature death, my hyphenated existence, and the pandemic – have taught me lessons that I would first store inside my body and mind, and later explore in my teaching and writing.

This collection is the result of pursuing my dream to be part of a community in which our backgrounds do not define us but in which we are also equally fluid and in constant interaction with so many other beautifully different people. Language matters to me immensely. I speak an accented, Balkan English, and I would not alter that for anything in the world! This collection has been designed in such a way to explore dramatic writing in English, as well as in translation. By so doing, we have a chance to listen to English and foreign sounds, opening the world's stage to infinite possibilities.

While the collection had several possible titles that morphed over time until reaching its current one, Thalia has always been a constant. On numerous occasions, I have been told that I have a "contagious laughter." During the awful year of 2020, that adjective resurfaced forcefully. It became imperative for me to try to laugh and think of ways to make other people laugh. Furthermore, while many people can say a few words about Dionysus, not many know about Thalia's existence, the goddess of comedy. In putting this collection together, I wanted to restore her name in an even more memorable way, as well as to acknowledge the hard work of women from around the world. "My" Thalia thus became *borderless* and, cliché as it may sound, laughter is undoubtedly universal. It makes us pause from all the tragedies in and around us by inviting us to enjoy the fleeting essence of life. It is through dance, poetry, and laughter that we create more durable and healthier communities.

FOREWORD | *Cătălina Florina Florescu*

I would like to thank all my contributors and translators for helping me laugh. When the world seemed to end, we stood up and fought against that through the healing power of comedic writing. The communal will to survive is universal.

On a personal note, I'd like to thank Mircea, my son, a rising senior at the Hudson School, whose artwork became the cover page. There were several possible images that we could have used. Given my professional background in Medical Humanities and my intimate relationship with loss and trauma, I did not want to opt for an image that had *any* relationship with the pandemic, in part because the title of the collection already addresses that, in part because humans are at first visual learners and later we become literate. To this day, we react differently to visual stimuli than we interact with language. Hence, I wanted something bold and full of life. When I asked for his permission, Mircea granted it easily; however, he wanted to "improve" the quality of the image, to make it look "smoother" and showed me an app that could do that. I *objected*. I wanted the artwork to speak *freely* about imperfection and thus to make all of us, whether we are artists or the general public, become self-aware of the invasive pressure that we have placed on our minds and bodies. We live in a world in which too many magazines still Photoshop images to project a dangerous fantasy that clearly does not exist. I hope that my son's unedited artwork gives us the courage to start the healing, by first admitting how deeply flawed we are, and yet to acknowledge that immense potential that many are too inhibited to share for fear their work is deemed not "perfect" and criticized harshly. I also want to thank all parents and guardians who had to find creative solutions during the tough months of the lockdown, followed by uncountable chaotic days of uncertainty that heavily affected our mental health. The silver lining of the pandemic was that it proved that the present *is* the time of our lives, that nothing is ever truly granted, that joy is a matter of authenticity, and that the arts are irrefutably palliative.

Thank you and enjoy reading our plays.

Cătălina Florina Florescu, Ph.D.
Hoboken, NJ, May 2022

You Are Muted

Christine Benvenuto

Cast

ISIS: in Egyptian mythology goddess of life and healing, protector of women and children; here, a therapist, fifties to sixties, any race/ethnicity

HORUS: in Egyptian mythology the son of ISIS and OSIRIS; here, their daughter, thirties to forties.

Time

The present.

Setting

Two Zoom screens located in the characters' homes. When characters are muted, their voices are audible but not to each other. If possible, the word "MUTE" appears on the screen.

HORUS: Good evening, Mother.
ISIS: Good evening, darling.
[*Both lift glasses*]
ISIS: Cheers!
HORUS: *Salute!*
ISIS: *Skal!*
HORUS: *Sei gesund!*
[*Both sip*]
ISIS: Mmmm. [*Inhaling*] That nose.
HORUS: That *taste*.
ISIS: I'm so glad you had the idea for us to buy the same wines. It's more like sharing a bottle than drinking alone in our self-isolation. [*Sips*] The children are asleep?
HORUS: They are.
ISIS: How are they?

HORUS: They're fine. They're managing. They're – they were used to him being away since the divorce anyway. This isn't much different for them.

ISIS: But it's entirely different.

HORUS: Of course it's different, Mother, in as much as absent from life is different from absent from home, which is different from absent minded. What they have in common is absence. Look. See these drawings? This one's from *before*. [*Holds up child's drawing depicting adult female and two children huddled at one edge of paper, male figure alone, opposite*] This one is *after*. [*Shows similar drawing with man horizontal, a corpse*]

ISIS: Oh, dear. Tragic.

HORUS: Yes, well. Honestly, we talk more about *you* than about him.

ISIS: Really? It's so hard to support children remotely. I wish I could do much more. I worry – sometimes I wonder if they really remember me. If they know who I am.

HORUS: Of course they remember you. They aren't idiots, Mother. They don't have dementia.

ISIS: With young children it's hard to know.

HORUS [*snaps*]: It's not hard to know with these children. They're not that young. They speak!

ISIS: Horus, darling, I know you're very angry.

HORUS: Angry? Angry. Am I angry?

ISIS: Well, I ...

HORUS: Look, they remember last summer. Well, no, I mean the summer before last. Yeah, it was a long time ago, wasn't it? Fucking COVID. But ... we look at all the photos we've taken with you. We talk about you about things we've done together.

ISIS: Thank you, darling.

HORUS: You can call them in the morning. I'll send you their online school schedules. But I'm with them all day. I have no life! I need to talk with you myself, while they're sleeping.

ISIS: Of course, I want that too. Tell me about you. How was your day?

HORUS [*sighs*]: No, let's talk about you for a change. You first, anyway. We end up spending every conversation on me. And there are things I want to know.

Christine Benvenuto | YOU ARE MUTED

ISIS: Ask whatever you'd like.

HORUS: Hmm. Well. One thing I've been thinking about my father, about Osiris. What was the real deal there? I mean, why did you marry him in the first place?

ISIS: Oh. [*Surprised; sits up very straight, begins reciting in stentorian tones*] I can't explain why she did this. Even though this girl is, or rather was, me. Isis married Osiris. In due time, a daughter was born to them ...

HORUS: Whoa, whoa, hold up. Why are you speaking this way? In the third person? Why are you – *intoning*?

ISIS: I'm a Greek chorus. It seems appropriate when I tell our family's story. I would invite members of our audience to take over the role of chorus, but then there are all those unpleasant echoes. You can do the Zoom applause, all of you out there! [*Demonstrates two-handed Zoom wave*]

HORUS: One person isn't a chorus.

ISIS: Adjustments must be made in a time of plague.

HORUS: Speak normally! Tell me. Why couldn't you pick someone – at least someone –

ISIS: Someone?

HORUS: Intact.

ISIS: Intact. You think your father wasn't intact? What does "intact" mean to you, darling?

HORUS: He was unbalanced. Deficient. I mean, he was a one-legged man. He had that pant leg hanging empty one side. With just a peg, a peg leg!

ISIS: Oh, my, we don't want to be offensive to one-legged men. Ablist.

HORUS: You couldn't dance!

ISIS [*muted*]: You're wrong, Sweetie. [*Smiles sadly*] We danced.

HORUS: Wait. Your lips are still moving but I can't hear you. You're muted. Did you just mute yourself? A silent chorus of one. There's something deeply, deeply –

ISIS [*unmuted*]: Personal?

HORUS: – strange about that. Wait. I thought you were muted.

ISIS: I've unmuted. Your father wasn't one-legged. You're displacing. I understand why, of course. [*Muted*] I mean he wasn't intact, not as a person. I think of Osiris now as someone whose

Borderless Thalia

YOU ARE MUTED | Christine Benvenuto

sperm I used to get pregnant. When you told me what he'd done …

HORUS: Wait! You're muted again!

ISIS [*unmuted*]: He was dead to me. I divorced him. Then oddly enough he *was* dead. Really dead. Drowned in a swimming accident. That's what the authorities concluded: an accident. They recovered the body. Most of it. They surmised the penis had been eaten by fish.

HORUS: What kind of fish eats a penis?

ISIS: I could answer that many ways. I think I'll choose to keep mute on that subject. But darling, it's not an empty pant leg flapping in the breeze that disturbs you. It's a symbol. The empty pant leg. You know, a symbol of something missing.

HORUS: As you've pointed out before, Mother, you aren't my therapist.

ISIS: No. I'm not. But I am the goddess of healing, and I am a therapist even if not *your* therapist. And it doesn't really take a therapist to deduce that what's troubling you is absence. Loss. Loss, darling. [HORUS *hums loudly*] Darling. Darling. [HORUS *hums louder*] Darling! [HORUS *stops humming*] You always hum. If I try to talk about loss, you begin humming. It's like when I tried to tell you what are colloquially referred to as the facts of life.

HORUS: Now you're trying to tell me the facts of death.

ISIS: I don't have to tell you those, my darling. I'm sorry to say you already know.

HORUS: Okay. We'd better cut this off right now. Haha. Cut off – no pun intended.

ISIS: It's painful but …

HORUS: No. We can't talk about him, or about my ex either, because then we fail The Test. If we talk about that fish-eaten penis, even, we fail. We don't pass The Test.

ISIS: Explain to me what this is again. The Test.

HORUS: I've told you.

ISIS: I know you've told me. Tell me again.

HORUS: It's a rule that when two women talk to each they have to talk about something besides a man. If they talk to each other about a man they fail The Test. It's become so oppressive. Just another way to shut women up, to clam up the mouths of two women who want to talk to each other about some asshole. You know who really benefits? The guy. The creep. The one whose assholic history with one woman doesn't get passed on, whose assholic treatment of his current girlfriend doesn't get talked about.

ISIS: I don't think –

HORUS: Yes, Mother, yes! Let's imagine this scenario: You run into the woman your husband got involved with after you.

ISIS: But your father's dead. He isn't with any other woman. Not to mention that after the fish ate his penis he wouldn't be up to much.

HORUS: I know that. Imagine, okay? This is hypothetical. You run into this woman and want to tell her what a creep she has on her hands. She wants to tell you what a creep she took off your hands. Her friends say it's not her fault everything's gone hopelessly wrong, but do they really know? If he was great to you, it could be her. But if she could talk to you, you'd be the best support in the world. And you'd get the chance to push all that weight off your chest too. You'd tell her, *Get the fuck out that relationship now! Nearest exit! ASAP!* You'd both be better off. But you can't have this conversation. Because even to have this conversation means failure. You. Fail. The. Test.

ISIS: But if the man is dead ...

HORUS: Fail!

ISIS: Hmm. If the two women are lesbians?

HORUS: Fail! No one's getting off that easily. Makes no difference whatsoever.

ISIS: We really can't talk about any man? Your boss? Donald Trump? Adolf Hitler?

HORUS: Correct. Especially my boss and Donald Trump and Adolf Hitler.

ISIS: Why?

HORUS: Because they're fuckers! Because The Test says it's pathetic if two smart, educated, multidimensional women such as ourselves sit here talking about the assholes who've done us wrong. And who's done worse – wronger – than those shits aforementioned?

ISIS: They are shits, darling, certainly. I do see what you mean. But I don't think the idea is to censor women. I imagine it's meant to encourage women to broaden our horizons.

YOU ARE MUTED | Christine Benvenuto

HORUS: Fuck horizons. Like I need someone telling me what are and shouldn't be my horizons? Like you do? Like either of us needs someone deciding what we're allowed to say?

ISIS: What if one woman is the therapist of the other woman?

HORUS: Fail! [*Muted*] Good point. They have to start policing therapists' sessions. We wouldn't want any woman getting away with failure.

ISIS: Unmute yourself, Honey. I missed that.

HORUS: I can't.

ISIS: What are you saying? I see your lips moving. You're saying you can't? You're nodding yes. Yes you can't unmute yourself or yes – yes? yes? Yes, you can't unmute yourself. Oh, good. I mean good I understand now. But why can't you?

HORUS [*unmuted*]: I can't unmute myself –

ISIS: You just did, I hear you now.

HORUS: I was muting myself because I'm bound to talk about something retro. Backward.

ISIS: Well, let's talk about something progressive, sweetheart.

HORUS: Okay, fine. Share your wisdom. You rise above it all. How do you do it?

ISIS [*intones*]: *Isis has achieved deep equanimity.*

HORUS: How, but? People are telling Isis – *you* their problems all day. How do you take it all in? What do you do after sessions with your clients? To unwind?

ISIS: Yoga. I've begun taking a yoga class. You were doing yoga at one point weren't you?

HORUS: I tried to be one of those yoga girls but I couldn't get the clothes right. The scarves – forget it.

ISIS: Scarves? I didn't realize there was scarf yoga. There's every kind of yoga these days. Yoga with animals – I don't like the sound of it. I hope it's not tantric yoga with animals.

HORUS: Mother. Please.

ISIS: People do all sorts of things. It could happen. Who are we to condemn?

HORUS: When it comes to bestiality it's okay to condemn. But the scarves aren't part of the yoga. Haven't you noticed how your teacher arrives for class? Oh, no, it's an online class. You'll have to take my word for it. The women who teach those classes have this superhuman ability to wrap their necks beautifully in huge scarves. Effortlessly. I either can't get the thing to stay on in the first place or I choke myself. And when I try to get it off I only make it tighter and tighter until I'm gasping for air. But these yoga gals think nothing of wrapping and unwrapping themselves. They look great, every one of them.

ISIS: Have you tried watching them?

HORUS: I've watched them. It's like juggling. Watching doesn't put the power in my hands.

ISIS: What will put the power in your hands?

HORUS: I don't know, Mother. I don't know.

ISIS: Do the male yoga teachers wear scarves? Because actually my teacher is a man.

HORUS: A man. A man yoga teacher.

ISIS: Yes. Startling, I know.

HORUS: Hmm. My guess is they do. But you'd have to see him outside to know for sure.

ISIS: I guess we should stop talking about him.

HORUS: Oh! [*Muted*] Right. Another male. Well, there goes yoga as a conversational topic. [*Unmuted*] But here we go talking about me again. We were supposed to talk about you. Instead you end up trying to help empower me.

ISIS: I would love to help empower you, Sweetheart. I've wanted to for such a long time. Not just now. This isn't the first time you've suffered, darling.

HORUS: It's not the first time anyone's suffered.

ISIS: I'm not thinking about "anyone," I'm thinking about you. Remember when you told me about your father? How he used to come into your bed at night and look at you? He never touched you, you said. Just looked.

HORUS [*sarcastic*]: I think I remember that, yes.

ISIS [*sighs*]: I wanted to take a scissors and snip his penis off when I heard that. He wasn't using his penis. Still. I figured his desire to stare at you sprang from that location. I called the police, the lawyers, the DA's office.

HORUS: You did?

YOU ARE MUTED | *Christine Benvenuto*

ISIS: Oh yes. I told them everything. Everyone refused to help us. They said unless he actually touched there was nothing they could do. That was just so wrong.

HORUS: So you divorced him.

ISIS: So I divorced him. And then the court said I had to let you see him. I thought he wouldn't dare try it again. I was wrong. You didn't tell me right away. You held it inside and then one night at dinner, you just casually spilled it. The whole story.

HORUS: I remember, Mother.

ISIS: The staring. Sleeping together in his bed when you had overnight visits. The shower. You remember the shower?

HORUS [*muted*]: I remember.

ISIS: You're muted again. But I know you remember. He said he would read to you while you showered so that he could be with you in the bathroom. Watching you. Who reads to a child in the shower? But you knew. You said there was a clear glass wall on his shower and he used it to look at your body while you washed.

HORUS [*unmuted*]: Oh – [*groans*] I remember. *Hmmmm*. So. After I told you about that, he went out and conveniently drowned? And the fish conveniently ate his penis. The penis you wanted to snip off. Huh?

ISIS: That's right. [*Silence*] I failed you. I failed to protect you.

HORUS [*getting upset*]: Mom, you're a goddess.

ISIS: That's why you're so angry. With me – for letting terrible things happen.

HORUS: You're the queen of goddesses!

ISIS: I know, honey. Even so. I failed you. I see you on the other side of that glass wall.

HORUS: I feel like screaming.

ISIS: Yes. You're on the other side of that glass shower wall. Your mouth is moving. You're – you're calling for help, maybe. Maybe telling him to leave you alone. Maybe screaming. But I can't hear you. I can't hear what you're saying.

HORUS: I'm muted.

ISIS: That's right. Muted.

THE END

Christine Benvenuto | YOU ARE MUTED

L'audio è disattivato

HORUS: Buona sera, Madre.
ISIS: Buona sera, tesora.
[*Entrambi alzano i bicchieri*]
ISIS: Salute!
HORUS: *Cheers!*
ISIS: *Skal!*
HORUS: *Sei gesund!*
[*Entrambi sorseggiano*]
ISIS: Mmmm. [*Inalazione*] Quel naso.
HORUS: Quel *sapore*.
ISIS: Sono così felice che tu abbia avuto l'idea per noi di acquistare gli stessi vini. È più come condividere una bottiglia che bere da soli nel nostro isolamento reciproco. [*Sorseggia*] I bambini dormono?
HORUS: Sono.
ISIS: Come stanno?
HORUS: Stanno bene. Stanno gestendo. Loro sono ... erano abituati al fatto che fosse assente dal divorzio comunque. Questo non è molto diverso per loro.
ISIS: Ma è completamente diverso.
HORUS: Naturalmente è diverso, Madre, in quanto assente dalla vita è diverso da assente da casa, che è diverso da distratto. Ciò che hanno in comune è l'assenza. Guardare. Vedi questi disegni? Questo è di prima. [*Regge il disegno del bambino raffigurante una femmina adulta e due bambini rannicchiati su un bordo di carta, figura maschile da sola, di fronte*] Questo è dopo. [*Mostra un disegno simile con l'uomo orizzontale, un cadavere*]
ISIS: Oh, cara. Tragico.
HORUS: Si, beh. Onestamente, parliamo più di te che di lui.
ISIS: Davvero? È così difficile sostenere i bambini da remoto. Vorrei poter fare molto di più. Mi preoccupo – a volte mi chiedo se si ricordano davvero di me. Se sanno chi sono.
HORUS: Naturalmente si ricordano di te. Non sono idioti, Madre. Non hanno demenza.
ISIS: Con i bambini piccoli è difficile saperlo.

HORUS [*infastidito*]: Non è difficile saperlo con questi bambini. Non sono così giovani. Parlano!
ISIS: Horus, cara, che sei molto arrabbiata.
HORUS: Arrabbiata? Arrabbiata. Sono arrabbiata?
ISIS: Bene, io –
HORUS: Ricordano l'estate scorsa. Beh, no, intendo l'estate prima dell'ultima. Sì, è stato molto tempo fa, non è vero? Cazzo di COVID. Ma – Guardiamo tutte le foto che abbiamo scattato con te. Parliamo di te, di cose che abbiamo fatto insieme.
ISIS: Grazie, tesora.
HORUS: Puoi chiamarli al mattino. Ti invierò i loro orari scolastici online. Ma io sto con loro tutto il giorno. Non ho vita! Ho bisogno di parlare con te, mentre dormono.
ISIS: Naturalmente, voglio anche questo. Parlami di te. Com'è andata oggi?
HORUS [*sospira*]: No, parliamo di per cambiare. Tu per primo, comunque. Finiamo per spendere ogni conversazione su di me. E ci sono cose che voglio sapere.
ISIS: Chiedi qualsiasi cosa.

Spell: A One-Act Riff in Verse on Shakespeare's *The Tempest*

Barbara Blatner

Cast

ARIEL: a spirit of Air, has magical powers, any gender
CALIBAN: a creature of Earth, any gender
PROSPERO: a once-powerful magician, now a tired old man.

Setting

A lush island, home to diverse beings, where the exiled PROSPERO and his daughter landed in *The Tempest*.

[ARIEL, *coughing, breathing with difficulty, sits or stands on the branch of a tree, looks at the sky.* CALIBAN *enters below, startling* ARIEL]
ARIEL: Caliban! Help me!
CALIBAN [*sardonic*]: Why do you cough so violently, Ariel? God forbid, you'll break your delicate bones.
ARIEL [*to* CALIBAN]: Stop your rancorous mouth, creature of dust. I'm made of light high above *your* ground.
CALIBAN [*insincere*]: Darling Ariel, delicate radiance, how can one so far beneath you help at all?
ARIEL: For once shut off resenting me and *do* something, wretch, I cannot – breathe!
CALIBAN: Haughty one, sincerely now, what can *I* do?
ARIEL [*pointing to the sky, coughing, etc.*]: Our island skies swarm blacker with hideous soot than even this morning! All my kin who live in air, mosquito, dragonfly and dove, gasp and heave, their babies take [*breathing hard*] no – full – breath, their eyes dull, and you –
CALIBAN: – I and my *Earth*-bound kin are just fine, thank you very much.

Borderless Thalia

SPELL | *Barbara Blatner*

ARIEL: You who live close to Earth will last a few hours more than me, but soon you too will lose this wave-skirted world you love, and life.
CALIBAN: Ash covers all your thoughts, Ariel, you speak of nothing else, you're obsessed.
ARIEL: Deny it all, but ash will eat *your* breath, coat *your* feet –
CALIBAN: Why do you always ruin my day, airhead?
ARIEL: I trouble you as doom approaches?! [*Coughs*]
CALIBAN: In a day or two, island winds will blow this smoke away.
ARIEL: Wrong, as usual. Why can't your Earth-bound mind look up? [*Gesturing to sky*]
CALIBAN: Why can't your light-stuffed eyes look down? Except on *me*. Why do you always snub me?
ARIEL: There's no time to think about that.
CALIBAN: I like to be liked. Everyone does.
ARIEL: Go away, if you won't help me. I can't inhale your grievances *and* this smoke.
CALIBAN: I'll tell you who's to blame for this sky.
ARIEL: So, you do *not* deny we near apocalypse?
CALIBAN: I deny nothing, not your suffering, not the tainting of our clouds. But I feel no hope, no wing of it flutters in my chest. We will perish, cousin, everyone in Earth, air and water. I tell you who's to blame, only *he* can mend our calamity. Why not come down to *my* level from your branch?
ARIEL: I'll stay right where I am.
CALIBAN: Wind for brains, you'll breathe easier nearer the ground.
ARIEL: Shut up and say who diseased our sky.
CALIBAN: It is your master, the [*sarcastic*] *great* magician Prospero who has corrupted our lungs.
ARIEL: Prospero?!
CALIBAN: The one you serve so cravenly.
ARIEL: *Served*, past tense. Just an hour ago he freed me from his dominance, as he promised. I will not hear you slander Prospero.
CALIBAN: He sickened our heavens!
ARIEL: He's done nothing but good the twelve years he and his daughter have lived here.

Barbara Blatner | SPELL

CALIBAN: Sad, you still worship the invader who bound your mind and spirit to him, enslaving *your* skills every second of those twelve years!

ARIEL: Stop throwing muddy grudges in my face or I will go!

CALIBAN: Don't go, Ariel! Give me a chance to know you – a bit better – and you know me.

ARIEL: This is no cocktail hour, you lump! [*Gesturing to sky*]

CALIBAN: I swear, it was a cursed day that devil Prospero washed on our sands in his rotten boat.

ARIEL: *I* praise every island god that Prospero landed here with his infant child, banished by callous enemies from Milan –

CALIBAN: – where he was, face it, Ariel, a dismal Duke who gave the finger to his job and immersed himself in the study of magic to Milan's detriment! No wonder he was exiled on the sea!

ARIEL: I will *never* forget it was Prospero who with his vast alchemy sprung me from my years of hell inside that pine! [*Pointing to nearby pine tree*]

CALIBAN: – shrieking like a headless crow.

ARIEL: And I will not forget it was *your* mother, the horrid witch Sycorax, who trapped me there because I would not with *my* magic craft carry out her scorching aims for our lush woods!

CALIBAN [*under his/her breath*]: I never liked my mother much, I confess.

ARIEL: *What* did you say?!

CALIBAN: You hate me because of my mother? I am *not* her, Ariel. [*Quick beat*] You will not speak? All right, so where's your divine magician now?

ARIEL: I met him by his cave an hour ago. He freed me for the final time. I have discharged all his commands and aptly tricked his enemies. Prospero sails home to Milan today. [*Coughing*] And I – am – free! Finally – I serve – no one!

CALIBAN: You're free to bust your lungs and die, all right. Prospero's to blame!

ARIEL: I will not bear that thought, I *cannot*.

CALIBAN: Airhead, you have a slave's heart.

ARIEL: What?

CALIBAN: A slave's heart! You.

SPELL | Barbara Blatner

ARIEL: Muckraker, *your* back was bent as much as mine to Prospero's desires.

CALIBAN: O no, I fought him with my feet, fingernails and brain. He never was *my* master.

ARIEL: Good for you.

CALIBAN: Every hour I fought the wizard, more potent than the gods of my mother, and withstood his punishments. I have scars. Here. Here. [*Shows scars on his hands, legs*]

ARIEL: I didn't know this. But here's the deal: Prospero loved me and not you.

CALIBAN: Oh, Prospero loved me at first, petted me like a child. I held to him, I was lonely, my mother had died, and I never had a father to name. But Prospero thought I *was* a child of no age in mind or experience.

ARIEL: I didn't know he *ever* loved you.

CALIBAN: You know so little of *my* life on this solid ground. I tell you, soon Prospero turned on me, forced me, like you, to labor.

ARIEL: He said you would put hands on his sweet daughter.

CALIBAN: So he said. But I loved father *and* daughter and both misread me, called me bad, because my ways, my face, my contents are so different from theirs.

ARIEL: This is a new point of view for me. I'll consider it – medium trustingly.

CALIBAN: That's – a start. But listen: All day long he made me chop our tall sunlit trees, lay out their bones to dry, then light monstrous fires dawn to dawn –

ARIEL: – to warm him and his child, cook their food, scare off tigers –

CALIBAN: – to use all he wanted of our woods for himself. The sky belongs to no one, you know that. Spirit, with his incessant fires your Prospero sent up poison ash, the poison breath that kills us now as we mourn our lost radiant blue.

ARIEL: I am – astounded. Caliban! We must stop this man before he sails, bequeathing wreckage! With his magic, so much greater than mine, he will cleanse our oxygen.

CALIBAN: Agreed. So, I have done something to help, Ariel? *Now* will your highness come down to Earth and meet my eye?

ARIEL: Oh, all right. [ARIEL *comes down from tree to ground, breathes better*] My breath's a little – looser here, it's true.
CALIBAN: We'll demand of Prospero he cure our breath for good.
ARIEL: You – you demand it, Caliban. I'll – stand by.
CALIBAN: No dice! He's not your master anymore.
ARIEL: Um – I – forgot.
CALIBAN: Here he comes.
[*Enter* PROSPERO *slowly, an old, somewhat feeble man with a cane and a hat on his head, carrying an old suitcase.* CALIBAN: *steps out of view,* ARIEL *steps forward*]
ARIEL [*to* PROSPERO]: Former master.
CALIBAN [*under his breath*]: Monster.
PROSPERO: My dear Ariel, I go now to my ship, Miranda and the others wait for me. I thought you and I said our goodbyes.
ARIEL: Magician, I am not well, I am ill with the infection of the clouds.
PROSPERO: I do not follow. *What* do you say?
ARIEL: My lungs suffer from this foul sky. [*Points to sky*]
PROSPERO: I don't know what you say. What primitive language do you speak? Speak in *my* tongue, the one I taught you when I came from Milan.
CALIBAN [*stepping forward*]: Prospero.
PROSPERO: Stay back, worm! Miranda's safe from you on the ship, but I – !
CALIBAN: Why do you cringe from me, potent one? You've never done *that* before. Where is your magnificent arrogance supreme?
PROSPERO: I don't grasp your words, they're cries wolves and owls make! [*To* ARIEL] *Are* you my Ariel or some hostile sprite who looks like her/him? Use *my* language, so I can parse you!
CALIBAN [*to* ARIEL, *bewildered*]: He understood our native language when he enslaved us.
PROSPERO: Whatever gibberish you speak, I leave far behind. Goodbye. [*Starts to exit to his ship*]
CALIBAN: We cannot let him leave! Tell him in *his* tongue to remedy heaven! [*Pointing to sky*] He'll listen more to you, not me.
ARIEL: Prospero, sir, before you go, will you – please, sir, listen to – to my plea?
CALIBAN: Polite, much?

SPELL | *Barbara Blatner*

PROSPERO: Ah, there's my gracious spirit. But what is it? My ship lies on the bay with swollen sails.

CALIBAN: Prospero, with your own syllables I'll make this clear: You killed our air with high, bloody fires. Now with your most stirring spells, transform it, let us live –

ARIEL: Reverse this – this disaster, ex-master, before you go, clear the deadly smog, or else all you leave dies behind you.

PROSPERO: Now I scan your words but not their sense. Disaster? *What* disaster? I have finished all my work on this soil. Do not try my patience! What disaster?!

CALIBAN: Up there!

ARIEL: There!

PROSPERO: Where, what is it?!

CALIBAN, ARIEL: The sky! [*Quick beat.* PROSPERO *looks at the sky*]

PROSPERO: What the hell is wrong with the sky?!

ARIEL: It roils with constant smoke! [*Has a coughing fit*]

CALIBAN: What the hell is wrong with your eyes?!

PROSPERO [*looking up*]: I see nothing but sheets of blue I saw the first day I arrived. I just don't follow you. This place I knew for many suns is suddenly alien. I am glad to go.

CALIBAN [*to* PROSPERO *about* ARIEL]: You don't see the billowing ash that burns his throat?!

PROSPERO [*points to the bay where his ship prepares to sail*]: They hoist my sails below! I make my way! [PROSPERO *continues to exit*]

ARIEL [*to* CALIBAN]: Poor man, he cannot *bear* to see what he has done.

CALIBAN: Poor man, are you kidding? He sees what he *will* see, nothing more.

PROSPERO: Talk all the nonsense you like! Goodbye! [*Beat.* PROSPERO *continues to EXIT*]

ARIEL: Wait, you can't go!

PROSPERO: Servant, yes you are free now but free to tell me what to do? Ariel, dream on. Ah, a catch in my throat. [*Coughs*]

[PROSPERO *continues to exit.* CALIBAN *grabs* PROSPERO, *drags him to the tree, starts to bind him there with a vine circling the tree*]

PROSPERO [*to* CALIBAN]: What are you – doing?!

CALIBAN [*to* ARIEL]: You wanted action, cousin?! Help *me* now, bind him!
PROSPERO: Let – me – go!
[ARIEL: *helps* CALIBAN *bind* PROSPERO, *but backs off*]
ARIEL [*wavering in resolve*]: Do I hurt you, master? I mean – [*to* CALIBAN] I can't – quite – do this. My righteousness says *do it*, my loyalty says *no*.
PROSPERO: What are you squawking against me?! I loved you, Ariel. How can you pounce on me with this criminal?!
CALIBAN: Make your will your own, Ariel, so it huffs no more in *his* breeze! [ARIEL *again helps* CALIBAN *to secure* PROSPERO *to tree*] There!
ARIEL: Caliban, he'll use his wizardry to presto unbind himself and bind *us* to the dust?
PROSPERO [*straining against his bonds*]: Why do you tie me?! I've done nothing wrong!
[*Quick beat*]
CALIBAN: Then conjure liberty with your trickster arts.
PROSPERO: But I – just let me – go! Ah! [*Straining at his bonds*]
CALIBAN: Restore our skies your fires defiled and I promise I'll untie you.
PROSPERO: This sky's a still lake of electric blue! I don't see what your problem is, but *I* can't help you [*coughs a little*].
ARIEL: Caliban, could his shaman know-how – be gone?
CALIBAN: Clearly, he no longer grasps our language.
ARIEL: When he came here he so quickly delved our speech –
CALIBAN: – just to win us. Then he wielded spells and stuffed down every citizen's throat *his* exotic language –
ARIEL: – forced syllables on me especially –
CALIBAN: – *and* me.
PROSPERO: You shame yourselves to speak that silly speech!
ARIEL: It's true, he catechized *his* nouns and verbs – and muffled ours.
PROSPERO: I'm an old man, I want to go home.
CALIBAN: Ariel, he debased our tongue, the beats and rhymes by which I knew myself, my body –
ARIEL: – words by which we know our creatures, plants, every living thing –

SPELL | *Barbara Blatner*

CALIBAN: – my own words turned smoky in my head –
ARIEL: – like our sky [*pointing to sky*].
PROSPERO [*indicating his bound hands*]: My hands – chafe and burn!
ARIEL: It is – good to speak *our* words again. With you.
CALIBAN: Yes? Well. Thank you, Ariel. Once strands of the Sun's fire streamed down through green lacy leaves, touched my face, warmed my skin. But *his* sentences taught me my inferiority.
ARIEL: He broke more than our sky.
CALIBAN: He so demoted Caliban, there's no light inside [*tapping chest*].
PROSPERO: I will be ill if you retain me here. It will be on *your* backs.
ARIEL: You cannot free yourself, once-sovereign Prospero?
PROSPERO: If only. If only I had not thrown away a little while ago – God help me – all my books and magic kits to the bottom of the sea! Ach, why did I tell *you* that?! You'll use it against me.
ARIEL: You buried in the sea your wand and all the tools you used for conjuring?!
CALIBAN: – and to invade us.
PROSPERO: I thought I did not need them anymore, those contrived potencies. I was – [*straining to get free*] – wrong! I should have kept my magic longer! Rebel spirit, I'd fling you back into your prison tree. Caliban, I'd toss *you* in that tick-infested swamp [*pointing to "swamp"*].
ARIEL: But I thought you were –
CALIBAN: – you thought he was – ?
ARIEL: – all-powerful.
PROSPERO: Ariel, I do not know you anymore. You've let this demon mislead you.
[CALIBAN *grabs* PROSPERO's *hat and puts it on his head*]
CALIBAN: So former master is now present slave, Prospero!
ARIEL [*summoning will, courage*]: – Now you'll do what *I* tell you to. Get your magic back any way you can and help us. Then you'll go.
PROSPERO: I plunged my powers in the drumming sea, I cannot get them back!

[CALIBAN *puts his hands on* PROSPERO's *shoulders,* PROSPERO *tries to shake off* CALIBAN's *hands*]
PROSPERO: Don't touch me! Monster!
CALIBAN [*to* ARIEL]: He calls me "monster," has from the first. But isn't *he* monster?
PROSPERO: There goes your claptrap words again!
ARIEL: He's deaf as metal to our tongue, his powers to decode it gone.
PROSPERO: I beg you, let me sail to Milan, city of my birth, and meet my final fate *there,* not here.
ARIEL: He who was no less than God of all he saw –
CALIBAN: – king of nature and of *our* nature. Oh, dirtily he lowered us all.
PROSPERO [*indicating* CALIBAN]: To think I showered mercy on you, fiend Caliban, and let you live.
ARIEL: I've taken slavery's poison into myself.
CALIBAN: And I the bitterness of a – failed fighter.
ARIEL [*to* PROSPERO, *yanking vine around* PROSPERO's *neck*]: Remaster your witchcraft, fix this mess!
PROSPERO: Ahhh!
CALIBAN [*to* ARIEL]: Cousin, give up, he's a *common* monster now.
PROSPERO [*coughing, choking a bit*]: Bring me – water.
ARIEL: He cannot turn time around and hoist his spells from the vast sea that rolls over?
CALIBAN: It rolls over his spells forever.
ARIEL: Caliban, we are dead.
CALIBAN: Banish him to where he's banished from! [CALIBAN *puts his hands around* PROSPERO's *neck*]
PROSPERO: Your hands pollute me! [*Tries to shake off* CALIBAN]
CALIBAN: Shut up, monster.
PROSPERO: How dare you call me what *you* are?!
ARIEL: *I* once called him "master," believed in his mastery.
PROSPERO: Come find me, daughter! My strength – is gone.
ARIEL: How will we scourge you for your sins, Prospero? Let you sail away and die a natural death in pretty Milan while this island dies of your unnatural plundering?
CALIBAN: Why not stay and die with us? I would not flinch when *you* hit the dust.

SPELL | *Barbara Blatner*

PROSPERO: What?!

ARIEL [*to CALIBAN*]: That's too easy, cousin. [*To PROSPERO*] And I will *not* breathe my last with *you* at my side.

PROSPERO [*to ARIEL*]: How *dare* you.

ARIEL [*to CALIBAN*]: With *you*, perhaps, cousin.

CALIBAN: Really, Ariel?

PROSPERO: God of my fathers, spare me these indignities.

ARIEL: Caliban, I am so shot through with despair, to delete him in myself [*tapping chest*] – I could – I would –

CALIBAN: Kill him now?

PROSPERO: Oh Lord.

CALIBAN: That's the spirit, spirit!

PROSPERO: Now your words make awful sense. Miranda, help me!

ARIEL [*to CALIBAN*]: Could uncorrupted Ariel do such a thing?

CALIBAN: You're no more pure than the creatures crouching on this dirt that you disdain. Get that stone, brain him to a bloody stew! [*Picking up and handing a nearby stone to ARIEL*]

PROSPERO: I will be murdered here?!

[*ARIEL picks up a heavy stone and holds it over PROSPERO's head. Beat*]

ARIEL: Give me some of your dense intent, Caliban, to do this deed.

PROSPERO: Ariel! I gave your everything I could, like a father, guarded you with my concern, gifted order and reason to your mind, renamed your lakes and valleys with my proper nouns!

CALIBAN [*to ARIEL*]: There's murder in you, never fear.

ARIEL: Is that true?

CALIBAN: No creature is without it.

PROSPERO: Ariel! I sprung you from endless death-in-life in that gouged pine! I fed you fresh, civilized ideas, raised high your groundless purpose!

ARIEL [*to CALIBAN*]: Cousin, you're right. Some howling rage calls my murderous will!

PROSPERO: Do not kill me, my Ariel!

[*ARIEL lowers the stone towards PROSPERO's head*]

CALIBAN: I have a delicate heart concealed in me, I can't look!

Barbara Blatner | SPELL

PROSPERO [*shields himself*]: Heaven help me! [*ARIEL brings down the rock towards PROSPERO's head*] Wait! What crimes do you accuse me of?!
[*ARIEL stops the rock just above PROSPERO's head*]
CALIBAN: That *is* the question, Prospero.
ARIEL: I cannot kill him, now he's asked it. [*Lowers rock*]
PROSPERO: Am I alive?!
CALIBAN: At least I won't have to wipe up his blood.
PROSPERO: Alive!
CALIBAN [*to ARIEL*]: He asked about crimes, didn't he, spirit?
ARIEL [*to PROSPERO*]: You made me your voice, arms, legs, hands, spoke me into riling a tempest from calm seas, false tragic drownings, loud illusions, deeds I despised. You laid your language on our island like a sword! I hate it all! [*Indicating CALIBAN*] You made *him* everything you hate in yourself –
CALIBAN: You killed the beauty of our speech that names the million gods of this paradise. [*Gestures to trees, etc.*] Worse, you deliver choking to our lungs.
[*Beat. All cough*]
ARIEL: You made our land a chamber where we'll die, then blind yourself to the death you've hung up there, everywhere and in us.
[*Beat. All cough*]
PROSPERO: If all that is – true, it is – hard – to see. Is it – true? [*Coughing, a little at first, then increasingly*] You will not – say? But you've said – so much, in *your* senseless tongue, in mine. You are – silent now? Does your – silence – say it's true? I don't know – if I can grasp this. I am an old – man, once mighty – magician, now ordinary and full – of – crimes? [*Struggling to breathe*] My – breath – what's wrong with my – breath? You who – hold me here, Ariel – Caliban, why can't I – breathe?
CALIBAN: We told you.
ARIEL [*pointing up*]: Look again, do you see now?
PROSPERO [*coughing*]: Oh. Oh no. I see – deadly curls of black blotting out – where is – where is the silent field of sky I saw each day – I lived in this – rocky place? Did I do that with – my fires? That's what – you said? And did I – take words from your mouths to sound – mine? If monsters are – bewildered old –

SPELL | *Barbara Blatner*

men, I – am one. [*Beat. All cough.* ARIEL *puts down the stone.* PROSPERO *prays*] Great magician of this – visible world, you have stopped – my violent death, I am grateful. Ariel, I thank you. But Miranda must worry – where I am. Can you – find it in your hearts to let me go?

[*Beat.* CALIBAN *and* ARIEL *look at* PROSPERO, *then at each other*]

CALIBAN: Cousin, let's throw out one who never did belong in any acre of our wilderness.

[ARIEL *unties* PROSPERO. CALIBAN *throws* PROSPERO's *hat back on his head.* PROSPERO, *stumbling, running, exits*]

ARIEL: Get thee gone.

CALIBAN: Farewell, monster!

ARIEL: Sail away with your reckless generations. [PROSPERO *is gone.* ARIEL *continues*] Goodbye, ex-master. Now I must goodbye – all that was mastered in *me*. Cousin, perhaps I have not justly read the pages of the magical book that is Caliban.

CALIBAN [*to* ARIEL]: Really? You – like me?

ARIEL: I – I like you.

CALIBAN: I'm sorry that my mother did you so much wrong. She was a wretched one, wounded in her bones. I tried to love her.

ARIEL: Thank you.

[*Beat.* ARIEL *and* CALIBAN *awkwardly looking at each other*]

CALIBAN: Um – what do we do now? Is death approaching?

ARIEL: Probably. Meanwhile, I don't quite – know how to be with you.

CALIBAN: I can't quite – look at you.

ARIEL: Cousin, are you – shy?

CALIBAN: A little. But now Prospero has bent his head a little in remorse, my smoky mind begins to clear.

ARIEL: I have disdained you and your shaggy kind, but feel some force of Earth entering here – [*touches heart*] a power swelling in myself. Earthy being, am I more like you than I have known?

CALIBAN: I've faulted your flickering mind, judged you lightweight, yet I need some of the light that kindles you, can I have it, spirit?

ARIEL: We can't survive with me flailing in air and you helpless on the ground, can we? Let's find our future, death or life, together.

Barbara Blatner | SPELL

CALIBAN: Wait! Can we summon magic of our own to save us? Maybe the future's in *your* magic. You *are* free to use it.
ARIEL: Is it true?
CALIBAN: You served that guy so long, you have forgotten you can act without him.
ARIEL: But I'm so out of practice of my own magic-making.
CALIBAN: *You're* the one who made the ocean leap and brought radiant delusions to confuse Prospero's enemies.
ARIEL: You're right. Before I was imprisoned, *I* enchanted this windy realm, casting harmless charms like mist to delight everyone. Could I do make my own magic again, to save us?
CALIBAN: You need no other voice than your own to rule you now.
ARIEL: But I won't act alone, as Prospero did. We must unite, Caliban.
CALIBAN: You sound my hope. Ariel, we must claim the shining coinage of our language so it gleams in our mouths once more –
ARIEL: – and say our syllables proudly to enchant our forests, sea and bays, reviving native powers all around. Caliban, shake off the grim pollution of your heart, take back your proud role in our society.
CALIBAN: I will stand firm, pronounce my free name: I am *no* one's shadow, I am Caliban, Caliban.
ARIEL: With *my* magic firing our endeavors, we'll find a way –
CALIBAN: – to sweep our skies of poison. *You're* master now, and every one of us will do *your* magic!
ARIEL: All of us with claws, teeth, wings, fins, buds, roots, flowers and leaves in these woods and bays and, of course, in this air, will manifest clear skies together.
CALIBAN: Ariel, call every spirit of our cherished isle from pine, rose and wave, call all you love and tell them in your weightless style how much we need each voice for our above. [*Points to sky*]
ARIEL: Call all that live on your rich ground, the wolf, the ant, hedgehog, snake, instruct each one with your wise heart, rebound to some collective action we will take –
CALIBAN: – to find a fix for what he broke.
ARIEL: Meanwhile, I'll hug the Earth, conserve breath, spirit rain to infiltrate the smoke –
CALIBAN: – and your sweet winds chase away death.

SPELL | *Barbara Blatner*

ARIEL: Our days of division now are past.

ARIEL, CALIBAN: Together we our sky spell cast.

[*Beat. We hear, at first, faintly, all the voices of the island speaking a beautiful language. The voices crescendo. Rain begins to fall, crescendos.* ARIEL *and* CALIBAN, *joyous in the rain, look up, dance, embrace, etc.*]

THE END

Vraja

CALIBAN: Stai! Oare ne va fi de ajuns doar dacă ne zicem nouă o vrajă? Poate viitorul depinde de vraja *ta*. Tu *eşti* liber să te foloseşti de ea.

ARIEL: E adevărat?

CALIBAN: De atâta timp eşti prizonierul acelui om că ai şi uitat că poţi exista şi fără el.

ARIEL: Dar nu mai ştiu dacă mai pot face o vrajă.

CALIBAN: *Tu eşti* cel care a făcut ca oceanul să ţopăie şi le-a sucit minţile inamicilor lui Prospero.

ARIEL: Aşa este. Înainte să fiu încarcerat, *am* reuşit să farmec acest tărâm şi să îi bucur pe alţii de magia mea. Oare voi putea să pun o vrajă care să ne salveze?

CALIBAN: Nu ai nevoie decât de puterea vocii tale.

ARIEL: Dar nu am acţionat singur, aşa cum nici Prospero n-a făcut-o. Trebuie să fim uniţi, Caliban.

CALIBAN: Ai dreptate. Trebuie să ne lăsam ghidaţi de farmecul vocii noastre –

ARIEL: – şi să silabisim cu putere ca să fermecăm pădurea, marea, golful, resuscitând puterile native care sunt de jur împrejurul nostru. Caliban, hai, nu te descuraja, asumă-ţi rolul de lider.

CALIBAN: Îmi voi rosti numele cu mândrie: Eu *nu* sunt umbra nimănui, sunt Caliban, Caliban.

ARIEL: Şi cu magia noastră pusă în slujba interesului nostru o să ne găsim calea proprie –

CALIBAN: – să salvăm cerurile de toxicitate. Voi sunteţi stăpâni aici şi toată lumea vi se va supune!

ARIEL: Toți împreună, cu dinții, cu ghearele, cu aripile, cu tot ce are natura aici și cu tot ce are cerul aici vom fi uniți și acționa împreună.

CALIBAN: Ariel, anunță-i pe toți spiridușii tăi, anunță-i pe toți cei pe care îi iubești și spune-le că acum mai mult ca niciodată avem nevoie de ei. [*Arată către cer*]

ARIEL: Spune-le tuturor animalelor, zi-le ce să facă pentru ca împreună să reușim –

CALIBAN: – și să reparăm ce acel om a stricat.

ARIEL: Între timp, o să îmbrățișez pământul, o să îmi menajez resursele, o să las ca ploaia să intre în fum–

CALIBAN: – și dragele tale vânturi să țină moartea cât mai departe de noi.

ARIEL: Vremea când acționam separat se încheie acum.

ARIEL, CALIBAN: Împreună cerul ne va răspunde vrajei.

[*Un moment. La început abia auzim vocile celor de pe insula vorbind într-o limbă diafană. Vocile se aud din ce în ce mai tare. Începe să plouă. Până și ploaia imită vocile și se intensifică. ARIEL și CALIBAN sunt extaziați, dansează și se îmbrățișează în ploaie, etc.*]

(Translated by Cătălina Florina Florescu)

A Thanksgiving to Remember

Sarah Congress

Cast

MARGERY: the mom, 50 years old. A human resources manager having a COVID crisis
BRANDON: the son, 21 years old. A junior at Temple University
JULIANA: the daughter, 22 years old. A senior at Boston University
ED: forties, MARGERY's lover. Truck driver and recovering addict.

Setting

The week of Thanksgiving, during the height of the COVID-19 pandemic. An apartment in Philly.

Act I

[*Lights up. An untidy apartment in Philly. Audio: Spanish lesson*]
SPANISH LESSON [*seductive male voice*]: *Hola guapa, guapo,* or whatever gender you are identifying with today.
[*MARGERY enters wearing a sheer, bright, tight outfit from Forever 21*]
MARGERY: Where is my lipstick?
SPANISH LESSON [*seductive male voice*]: Time for Spanish lesson *numero ochenta y cinco*. Relax, have a drink. If you're over 21.
MARGERY [*laughing*]: How did the lipstick get into the compost bin? [*Stops smiling*] What did we *do* last night?
[*MARGERY washes off the tube of lipstick*]
SPANISH LESSON [*seductive male voice*]: Let this phrase rub over you like aloe vera: *Da miedo afuera.* [*Beat*] *Da miedo afuera.* [*Beat*] Repeat that.
MARGERY [*flirtatiously*]: *Da miedo afuera.*
SPANISH LESSON [*seductive male voice*]: *Bueno guapa/guapo/ other.*
MARGERY [*pleased with herself*]: Do I sound like I'm Spanish?

SPANISH LESSON [*seductive male voice*]: *Da miedo afuera* means: it's scary outside!
[*MARGERY unscrews a bottle of wine*]
SPANISH LESSON [*seductive male voice*]: *Si. Si. Si. Si. Si.* You'll be fluent in no time!
[*MARGERY pours herself a large glass of wine*]
MARGERY: How do you say, "Hope the kids get along with my new lover," in Spanish?
[*Front door opens. MARGERY turns off the Spanish lesson*]
MARGERY: Brandon honey? Is that you?
WOMAN'S VOICE [*offstage*]: No.
[*JULIANA appears with a large bag of laundry. She wears a face mask*]
JULIANA: Your other child.
MARGERY: Juliana. [*Staring at her daughter*] Have you lost weight?
JULIANA: Why?
[*MARGERY smooths her hands over her tight outfit*]
MARGERY: I'm on a cleanse.
JULIANA: With wine?
MARGERY: Wine, apricots, and celery. So close to fitting back into my old jeans.
JULIANA: What are you wearing?
MARGERY: Forever 21. Like it?
JULIANA: Can see your bra. [*Pointing to the kitchen table*] Whose denim jacket is that?
MARGERY: Give Mommy a hug.
[*JULIANA freezes*]
JULIANA: Haven't you been watching the news?
MARGERY: Big fan of Dr. Fauci. He's more famous than Oprah!
JULIANA: What if somebody sneezed on my roommate in circus skills class, and then she touched my loofah in the shower, and now I'm a COVID-19 disease vector?
[*Silence*]
JULIANA: Can't kill you on Thanksgiving.
[*Silence*]
MARGERY: Did I tell you that I'm taking Spanish lessons?
JULIANA: Mom. Put your mask on.

A THANKSGIVING TO REMEMBER | *Sarah Congress*

MARGERY: Someone sounds cranky from their drive. Fix you right up.
[*MARGERY pours Juliana a glass of wine*]
JULIANA: It's the middle of the afternoon.
MARGERY: In France they're already drunk.
JULIANA: This isn't France. This is Philly.
MARGERY [*topping off her glass*]: Woo! Who says human resource managers can't have fun?
JULIANA [*quietly*]: Doesn't mean you should get wasted before lunch.
MARGERY: Sweetheart, Boston University is too expensive to have germs. Sit down. Girl talk.
[*MARGERY sits on the couch. JULIANA sits as far as possible from MARGERY*]
MARGERY: How nice. Mother and daughter. Sitting on the couch.
[*JULIANA smiles uncomfortably*]
MARGERY: Juliana, do you ever feel like you're going crazy?
JULIANA: Mom, are you doing okay here alone without us?
MARGERY: Don't be silly honey, you kids left for school years ago.
JULIANA: ... without Dad?
[*Front door opens. BRANDON appears with a large bag of laundry. He wears a face mask*]
BRANDON: Temple has the worst lint screens.
MARGERY: My baby boy.
JULIANA: Never been so glad to see anyone. Ever.
BRANDON: Mom. Where's your face mask?
MARGERY: What is it with you kids and these masks?
BRANDON: Juliana and I are coming from big universities. We could infect you.
JULIANA: Kill you.
[*BRANDON picks up his bag of laundry*]
BRANDON: Maybe Thanksgiving was a bad idea.
[*JULIANA picks up her bag of laundry*]
JULIANA: Brandon's right.
MARGERY: But you just got here.
BRANDON: It's for your own protection, Mom.
JULIANA: And ours.

MARGERY: NEITHER OF YOU ARE GOING ANYWHERE. YOU'RE MY CHILDREN. IT'S A FUCKING NATIONAL HOLIDAY.

[*A thud is heard from upstairs*]

JULIANA: What was that?

MARGERY: Hmmm?

BRANDON: That loud thud?

JULIANA: Is someone upstairs?

MARGERY: Squirrel infestation.

[*Another thud is heard*]

BRANDON: Must be some pretty obese, definitely rabid, squirrels ...

[*MARGERY walks to the fridge*]

MARGERY: Who's hungry?

[*BRANDON pokes his head up the stairs*]

BRANDON: I had a premonition this place was haunted.

[*MARGERY pulls out a container*]

MARGERY: Leftover Chinese orange chicken from Happy Rainbow Dragon?

BRANDON [*checking over his shoulder*]: Like in *The Conjuring*.

JULIANA: I'm a vegetarian.

MARGERY: Still?

[*JULIANA nods*]

MARGERY: Still a lesbian too?

JULIANA: Could we *not* do this now?

BRANDON: Six feet.

[*BRANDON takes out a tape measure from a kitchen drawer. He measures out six feet from his arm to MARGERY's arm and from his arm to JULIANA's arm*]

BRANDON: Phew.

MARGERY: The condo is *not* haunted, nobody has COVID, and I'm doing fine here by myself.

[*MARGERY takes out a bottle of Clorox spray. She sprays the room*]

MARGERY [*to BRANDON*]: There. [*To JULIANA*] Satisfied?

BRANDON: Missed a spot over –

MARGERY: Now can we have a NICE THANKSGIVING?

BRANDON: Whose denim jacket is that?

[*Suddenly from offstage we hear a man singing*]

A THANKSGIVING TO REMEMBER | *Sarah Congress*

MAN'S VOICE [*offstage singing Bobby Darin's "Mac the Knife"*]: "Oh the shark, babe …"
[*JULIANA pulls out a bottle of mace from her purse*]
JULIANA [*whispering/pointing up*]: There's an intruder.
BRANDON: … Spirit.
MARGERY: Kids: do not panic.
[*MAN'S VOICE continues singing "Mac the Knife"*]
BRANDON [*whispering to ghost*]: We can hear you. Can you hear us?
MARGERY: Juliana, put down the mace.
BRANDON [*whispering to ghost*]: Did you die from COVID? Knock twice if you did.
[*MAN'S VOICE continues singing*]
JULIANA [*pulling out her phone*]: Calling the police.
MARGERY [*to JULIANA*]: Stop dialing the police. Ed sings in the shower sometimes.
JULIANA: Ed?
BRANDON [*quietly*]: The patriarch ghost …
[*The singing stops; the shower stops*]
JULIANA: Mom, who is Ed?
BRANDON [*quietly*]: What is Ed? ET, apparition, demon …
MARGERY: Ed is the truck driver I met at the Walgreens.
BRANDON: Oh.
JULIANA: Why is Ed from Walgreens using our shower?
MARGERY: Because children: Ed is my lover.
[*MARGERY pops open a fresh bottle of wine*]
MARGERY: That's right. I've taken a lover.
BRANDON: Is he staying for Thanksgiving?
JULIANA: Mom that's not okay.
[*MARGERY pours herself a glass of wine*]
MARGERY [*drinking*]: Both of you are really missing out.
JULIANA: You can't just shack up with some truck driver –
[*BRANDON goes to put his arms around MARGERY. JULIANA blocks his arm*]
JULIANA: Six feet Brandon.
[*BRANDON backs up*]
BRANDON: Six feet.

MARGERY: Ed is not just [*to* JULIANA] "some truck driver" [*to* BRANDON] "from Walgreens."
BRANDON: Is he from Tinder?
JULIANA: Brandon.
MARGERY: Ed is my soulmate.
[*ED appears. He speaks with a thick Texan accent*]
ED: Knock, knock.
[*ED points to* JULIANA]
ED: You must be Juliana.
[*ED points to* BRANDON]
ED: You must be Brandon.
[*ED points to* MARGERY]
ED: Know who you are.
[*ED grabs* MARGERY *by the waist and tickles her*]
MARGERY [*giggling*]: Ed, stop. That tickles.
ED: This spot? This spot? [*To* BRANDON/JULIANA] It's okay kids. I'm her COVID pod.
[MARGERY *and* ED *make out.* JULIANA *and* BRANDON *give each other desperate looks*]
ED [*to* BRANDON/JULIANA]: Know what you both are thinking.
JULIANA [*quietly*]: Couldn't possibly ...
[*ED takes a seat*]
ED: Who is this big guy with the Texan accent groping my mom?
[*ED props his feet up on the table*]
ED: First, let me tell you the story of who this big guy *used* to be.
BRANDON: Should probably start my laundry ...
ED: Laundry can wait. I was a sinner. A fornicator. An alcoholic. An opioid addict. A se –
MARGERY: So poetic.
ED: I would shoot up every night with Felix. [*To kids*] My drug dealer. Good man. Great cook.
BRANDON [*whispering to* JULIANA]: Why does it feel like we're in a Stephen King story?
JULIANA [*whispering to* BRANDON]: Because we are.
ED: Lied, cheated. Lost my wife. She didn't die – just lost her. Literally. Can't find her ... or the Bank of America Travel Rewards credit card.
MARGERY: So brave.

A THANKSGIVING TO REMEMBER | *Sarah Congress*

ED: But all that changed the day I met the Big Man. [*Beat*] Know who I mean?
JULIANA: AA sponsor?
BRANDON: Parole officer?
ED: Buddha. Met Buddha. [*Salutes the sky*] Thank you Buddha. Thank you, sir.
MARGERY: So inspiring.
ED: Buddha taught me that happiness can't be found in heroin or a Krispy Kreme donut. Happiness it comes from inside. Been sober and out of jail for the past seven and a half months ... give or take a month or two.
MARGERY: Keep telling him to apply for TedX Philly.
BRANDON [*to JULIANA*]: What the hell, 2020?
[*Lights out*]

Act II. The kitchen, later that night

[*JULIANA and BRANDON sit together at the kitchen table dressed in sweatpants looking at their laptops*]
BRANDON: According to Reddit, COVID mid-life crisis romances are super common.
JULIANA: Brandon, this is not a romance. He's using Mom.
[*MARGERY enters, dressed in Victoria's Secret nighttime attire*]
BRANDON [*covering his face*]: Burning eyes.
JULIANA: Mom tie your robe.
[*MARGERY ties her robe. She opens up a bottle of wine*]
MARGERY: What you kids doing?
BRANDON/JULIANA: Homework.
MARGERY: Wine?
JULIANA: Mom, do you have any background information on Ed?
MARGERY: We're in love. That's all the background info I need.
BRANDON: Does he have siblings; did he complete high school – ?
JULIANA: Is he wanted in any states?
MARGERY: He's a Buddhist.
[*Silence*]
MARGERY: We both enjoy watching *The View*.
JULIANA: And it's a monogamous relationship?
MARGERY: Yes ... pretty sure ...

BRANDON: And he doesn't have COVID?

MARGERY: Who's sure that any of us don't have COVID? This table could have COVID.

JULIANA: Mom, that's not how the disease is transmitted.

MARGERY: Your hoodie could have COVID.

JULIANA: Really need to start listening to NPR.

MARGERY: I'm happy. For the first time since your father dumped me I'm happy.

BRANDON: Mom, we just don't want you to get hurt.

[ED enters]

ED: Hallmark moment. Makes me wish I could spend Thanksgiving with my kids in Seattle.

MARGERY: You have kids?

ED: Let's go on up to bed skunk. [To BRANDON and JULIANA] Big day tomorrow. Lots to cook.

[ED and MARGERY exit. Lights dim on the kitchen. Lights up on the bedroom]

MARGERY: Didn't know you had kids, Ed.

ED [turning up the TV volume]: Bless what remains of my liver – favorite episode of *Schitt's Creek*.

MARGERY: So, when you're not here –

ED: Moira Rose. Margery, this here is the best actress in all of television.

MARGERY: Are there any other women that you "see"?

ED: "The world is falling apart around us, and I'm dying inside." Love me some Moira.

[MARGERY *gets out of bed. She walks into the bathroom. She turns on a Spanish lesson*]

SPANISH LESSON [*seductive male voice*]: *Buenos noches*. Welcome to Spanish *en la oscuridad*.

MARGERY: How do you say: "I'm having a COVID-19 existential crisis" in Spanish?

SPANISH LESSON [*seductive male voice*]: *Pijama. Pijama.* Now you try.

[*Lights out*]

A THANKSGIVING TO REMEMBER | Sarah Congress

Act III. Thanksgiving Day

[ED *drinks a beer and shucks peas.* Schitt's Creek *plays in the background.* BRANDON *enters*]

ED: Bless them sumbich's at TBS, those geniuses got a *Schitt's Creek* marathon playing on Thanksgiving Day. Yeehaw.

BRANDON: Ed?

ED: Beer?

BRANDON: Not before orange juice ... besides, aren't you in AA?

ED: Yup. But not for beer.

[ED *grabs himself another beer from the fridge*]

ED: Bird's already in the oven. Can you skin those potatoes over there? Gonna deep fry 'em in bacon rinds like Step-MeeMaw taught us.

BRANDON: Delicious. Have you seen –

ED: I ain't no goddamn baker.

BRANDON: ... No one accused you of being one?

ED: Ain't going bake no goddamn pie.

BRANDON: Listen, Ed where's –

[JULIANA *enters*]

JULIANA: Guys, have you seen Mom?

[ED *goes back to shucking peas*]

ED: No I have not seen your mother. Something wrong with that woman.

JULIANA: Clearly.

BRANDON: Yeah ...

ED: She doesn't like *Schitt's Creek*.

BRANDON [*looking at his phone*]: Turn on the news.

[JULIANA *turns on the news*]

FEMALE NEWS ANCHOR VOICE OVER: We now share footage from earlier this morning of 50-year-old human resources manager Margery Williams who was found dumping garbage bags full of Forever 21 clothing and empty wine bottles off the Betsy Ross Bridge.

[MARGERY *appears at the end of the stage holding a large garbage bag, scattering clothing out into the audience*]

MARGERY [*to the audience*]: Good morning Delaware River!

MALE NEWS ANCHOR VOICE OVER: Looks like someone's having a rough Thanksgiving.
FEMALE NEWS ANCHOR VOICE OVER: A police car stopped to question Ms. Williams on the bridge.
MARGERY [to the audience]: Had to do it. These things, they belong to the pandemic. Not to me.
ED: Is she throwing my denim jacket off the Betsy Ross Bridge?
FEMALE NEWS ANCHOR VOICE OVER: The police escorted Ms. Williams off the bridge. She may be facing criminal charges.
MARGERY [to the audience]: I may? Guess I might. [Shaking her head] 2020.
MALE NEWS ANCHOR VOICE OVER: Maybe next time she'll just donate to her local Buffalo Exchange.
[NEWS ANCHORS laugh. BRANDON turns the news off]
ED: Now she'll be wanting to be bailed out.
JULIANA: I'll go get Mom.
[JULIANA looks at her phone]
JULIANA: Mom's calling.
[MARGERY stands at the edge of the stage]
MARGERY [on the phone]: Juliana?
JULIANA [on the phone]: Mom? We just saw you on the news.
MARGERY [on the phone]: How did I look?
BRANDON [on the phone]: Crazy.
MARGERY [on the phone]: Yeah ... sorry ... [Beat] I'm actually outside.
JULIANA [on the phone]: You're what?
BRANDON: She's what?
[ED opens the oven to look at the turkey]
ED: Horse hockey – this bird ain't never gonna be done.
[ED slams the oven door shut]
MARGERY [on the phone]: Probably shouldn't come inside.
JULIANA [on the phone]: You have to come inside.
MARGERY [on the phone]: But what if I have COVID? The police station ...
[Silence]
BRANDON: We'll all wear masks.
[BRANDON and JULIANA put their face masks on and glare at ED. After a long pause ED puts his mask on]

A THANKSGIVING TO REMEMBER | *Sarah Congress*

MARGERY [*on the phone*]: Okay, I'm coming in.
[*The front door opens and* MARGERY *enters weary but strong*]
MARGERY: Ed, our fairy tale is at an end. Married your kind once. I'm not going to do it again.
ED: What about the turkey?
MARGERY: Fuck the turkey.
ED: Baby, you don't mean that.
MARGERY: Fuck. The. Turkey.
[ED *takes the turkey out of the oven. He throws it on the floor*]
ED: Turkey. Is. Fucked. [ED *tries to grab* MARGERY]
MARGERY: Six feet, Ed.
ED: Don't have to tell me twice.
[ED *exits*]
BRANDON: Wow. Mom.
MARGERY: I'm an outlaw. [*After a beat*] I do have to do some community service.
JULIANA: Glad to have you back.
BRANDON: Missed you. [MARGERY *sits*]
MARGERY: Sorry. I seem to have completely lost my mind.
JULIANA: Pretty normal during a global pandemic.
BRANDON: Should we order Chinese?
[MARGERY *nods.* BRANDON *picks up the phone while* JULIANA *scoops up the turkey remains*]
MARGERY: Did I tell you kids that I've been learning Spanish?
BRANDON [*on phone*]: Happy Rainbow Dragon? We'd like an order of chicken fried rice.
MARGERY: *Esta es mi familia.*
JULIANA: Brandon: *two* orders of veggie steamed dumplings.
MARGERY: *Esta es mi familia.*
BRANDON [*on phone*]: Singapore noodles.
JULIANA: Crab rangoon for Mom.
BRANDON [*on phone*]: Three orders of crab rangoon.
MARGERY: *Esta es mi familia.*
BRANDON [*on phone*]: Two hot and sour soups –
JULIANA: Fortune cookies and extra duck sauce.
MARGERY: This is my family.

THE END

Un Día de Acción de Gracias para Recordar

Personages: Dos Mujeres y Dos Hombres

Los papeles en esta obra de teatro pueden sen actuados por actores de cualquier raza o etnicidad.

MARGERY: la mamá, 50 años. Gerente de recursos humanos en medio de una crisis de COVID

BRANDON: el hijo, 21 años. Estudiante de tercer año (o junior) en la Universidad Temple

JULIANA: la hija, 22 años. Estudiante de último año (o senior) en La Universidad de Boston

ED: años cuarenta. El amante. Chofer de camiones y adicto en recuperación.

Dia de Acción de Gracias, 2020.

Apartamento en Philly (Filadelfia). Siempre, menos es mas.

[*Un apartamento desordenado en Filadelfia. Audio: una clase de español*]

CLASE DE ESPAÑOL [*una seductiva voz de hombre*]: Hola guapa, guapo, o cualquier género con el cual te estes identificando hoy.

[*MARGERY entra vestida en un conjunto transparente, brillante y apretado de PorSiempre 21*]

MARGERY: ¿Dónde está mi lápiz de labios?

MARGERY [*riéndose*]: ¿Cómo fue que el lápiz de labio se metió en la basura? [*Para de reír*]. ¿Qué *hicimos* anoche?

[*MARGERY lava el lápiz de labio*]

CLASE DE ESPAÑOL: Deje que esta frase le pase por la piel como si fuese aloe vera. [*Un latido*] Da miedo afuera. [*Un latido*] Da miedo afuera. [*Un latido*] Repítalo.

MARGERY [*coquetamente*]: Da miedo afuera.

CLASE DE ESPAÑOL: Bueno guapa/guapo/otro.

MARGERY [*contenta con sigo misma*]: ¿Sueno como si fuera española?

A THANKSGIVING TO REMEMBER | Sarah Congress

CLASE DE ESPAÑOL: *Da miedo afuera* quiere decir: que da miedo afuera!

[*MARGERY abre una botella de vino*]

CLASE DE ESPAÑOL: Si. Si. Si. Si. Si. ¡Muy pronto estarás hablando fluidamente!

[*MARGERY se sirve un vaso grande*]

MARGERY: ¿Cómo se dice en español: "Espero que a los muchachos les caiga bien mi nuevo amante"?

[*Se abre la puerta de enfrente. MARGERY apaga la clase de español*]

MARGERY: Brandon, cariño. ¿Eres tú?

VOZ DE MUJER [*fuera del escenario*]: No.

[*JULIANA entra cargando una bolsa grande de ropa sucia. Tiene puesta una máscara*]

JULIANA: Tu otro/a hijo/a.

MARGERY: Juliana. [*Mirando fijamente a su hija*] ¿Has perdido peso?

JULIANA: ¿Por qué?

[*MARGERY le pasa las manos por arriba a su apretado vestido*]

MARGERY: Estoy pasando por una limpieza.

JULIANA: ¿Con vino?

MARGERY: Vino, albaricoques y apio. Estoy que ya casi entro en mis jeans (o pantalones vaqueros) viejos.

JULIANA: ¿Que tienes puesto?

MARGERY: Por Siempre 21. ¿Te gusta?

JULIANA: Puedo ver tu sostén. [*Señalando a la mesa de la cocina*] ¿De quien es esa chaqueta/chamarra?

MARGERY: Dale un abrazo a mami.

[*JULIANA se congela*]

MARGERY: ¿No le puedo dar un abrazo a mi hija?

JULIANA: ¿No has estado mirando las noticias?

MARGERY: Soy una admiradora del Doctor Fauci. ¡Es más famoso que Oprah!

JULIANA: ¿Qué pasaría si alguien estornuda encima de mi compañera de cuarto en la clase de técnicas circenses, y después ella toca mi esponja de lufa en la ducha y ahora yo soy un vector del COVID-19?

[*Silencio*]

JULIANA: No te puede matar ... no en el Día de Acción de Gracias.

Quarrel-tine

Connie Dinkler

Cast

RACHEL: wife of WESLEY, mid-forties, vain, angers easily
WESLEY: husband of RACHEL, mid-forties, seemingly very anxious
EVAN: son of RACHEL and WESLEY, seventeen years old, calm, easy-going.

Setting

March 2020 in North Carolina, the living room of a modern home. There is a sofa, a coffee table in front of the sofa and a chair to the right of the sofa. There is a window behind the sofa.

At Rise

[WESLEY *is sitting on the sofa spraying the table with disinfectant and wiping it down.* EVAN *is reclining in the chair, scrolling on his phone, occasionally texting, rarely looking up from his phone. We hear a door shut.* RACHEL *enters stage left, her purse in her hand*]
WESLEY: Hey hon.
RACHEL: It is crazy seeing the streets so empty. [*She plops the purse down on the table*] And I can't believe the nail salon is closed!
[WESLEY *looks down at her purse, picks it up and wipes it off, then wipes the table again*]
RACHEL: I need a fill-in! [RACHEL *sighs and sits down on the sofa next to* WESLEY]
WESLEY [*worriedly*]: Did you wash your hands when you came in?
RACHEL: Yes! What do you think reminded me of how ugly my nails are!
WESLEY: Oh honey, they're not that bad. Did you wash your hands long enough? You're supposed to wash them for at least 20 seconds.

QUARREL-TINE | *Connie Dinkler*

RACHEL [*irritated*]: Yes, Wesley, I washed my hands for 20 seconds.

WESLEY: How do you know? Did you sing the happy birthday song? You're supposed to sing the happy birthday song twice while washing your hands that way you know you washed them long enough.

EVAN: Yeah, Mom. The happy birthday song.

RACHEL: Wesley! Lay off! Geez, what is wrong with you? You were already a little bit of a hypochondriac before this stupid Coronavirus thing and now you are ten times worse!

EVAN: Yeah, Dad. Chillax.

WESLEY: I am not a hypochondriac. I'm just trying to keep us all safe.

RACHEL: Safe from what? They are just blowing things all out of proportion. I doubt there even is a Coronavirus. It's all just a government conspiracy.

WESLEY: What are you talking about? Everything is a conspiracy to you. I read on the CDC webpage –

RACHEL: OMG! Quit spending all your time researching the COVID-19 case count!

WESLEY: Alright. Let's just agree to disagree here. [*Pause*] Were you able to find eggs?

RACHEL: Yes. I had to wrestle a four-eyed millennial to get them, but I got us some eggs.

WESLEY: Did you sanitize the shopping cart?

RACHEL: Wesley!

WESLEY: Okay, sorry.

RACHEL: Why is it I always have to do the grocery shopping anyway?

[*WESLEY wipes down the legs of the table*]

WESLEY: Because every time I do, you complain that I didn't get the right stuff.

RACHEL: That's because you don't get the right stuff! I write it all out in detail for you! Even an idiot couldn't mess up but somehow you end up messing it up every time.

WESLEY: You're just too picky.

RACHEL: I must not be too picky, I married you didn't I? You're just too lazy to take the time to read the list. What have you been doing while I was out running all the errands? Evan, don't be like your father when you get married and let your wife do everything.

EVAN: 'Kay, Mom.

WESLEY: I been disinfecting the house for one –

RACHEL: Again?

WESLEY: And I was just watching a special news report. The governor is putting in a stay-at-home order for North Carolina.

RACHEL [*sarcastically*]: Oh, that's just wonderful.

WESLEY: We are not supposed to leave our house now except to go to the pharmacy or get food. All businesses are shutting down except ones they are considering essential.

RACHEL: So I'm not going to be able to get my mani-pedi?

WESLEY: Nope.

RACHEL: Or go to the tanning bed?

WESLEY: Nope.

RACHEL: I can't go to the movies or to dinner with my girlfriends?

WESLEY: Nope.

RACHEL: What the heck can I do? I can't even go to work now at least then I could get away.

WESLEY: You can still go to the store to buy what you need to cook us dinner.

EVAN: Yeah, Mom.

RACHEL [*sarcastically*]: Oh that's fun.

WESLEY: Rachel, it won't be so bad. [*WESLEY reaches under the table and pulls out face masks*] Look! I made us matching monogrammed face masks!

RACHEL: Seriously?

WESLEY: I made one for Fido too.

RACHEL: You made the dog a monogrammed face mask?

WESLEY: Yes, but I think I may have to make some adjustments on his. I wasn't sure how to get the straps to go over his ears, but I'm working on it.

RACHEL: You're killing me.

WESLEY: No, but Covid-19 will kill you if you don't wear one of these.

[*RACHEL puts her hand on her forehead and sighs*]

WESLEY: You touched your face Rachel.

RACHEL: What?

QUARREL-TINE | *Connie Dinkler*

WESLEY: You just touched your face. Now you need to wash your hands.

RACHEL: I just washed my hands when I came in! I don't need to wash them again!

WESLEY: It doesn't matter, you should still wash your hands. You shouldn't be touching your face Rachel. They say COVID-19 can live up to three days on surfaces!

RACHEL [*angrily*]: You just said you have been disinfecting the house!

WESLEY: Yeah but I haven't got to every single surface yet.

RACHEL: OMG! I can't be here with your hypochondriacal self 24/7!

WESLEY: I'm sorry dear. I guess I get a little overly protective. Remember, we are in this together. [*WESLEY starts spraying the sofa with disinfectant*] Aren't you going to try your mask on?

RACHEL: I'm not putting that thing on! It will mess up my make-up! Do you know how long it takes me to put my makeup on?

WESLEY: Absolutely I do. Are you really worried about your make-up when people are dying?

RACHEL [*frantically*]: Dying – that reminds me! [*RACHEL runs her fingers through her hair*] I have to get my roots done soon! What am I going to do?

EVAN: You touched your face again, Mom.

RACHEL: Evan, you're grounded.

EVAN: 'Kay, Mom.

WESLEY: You're incredible. As always, only thinking of yourself. Why would I think a pandemic would change that. Why can't you just color your hair at home?

RACHEL: At home? From a box? Seriously?

WESLEY: You are more concerned about your hair than the poor hairdressers that are now out of work with no money to feed their families. How can you be so selfish?

RACHEL: Me selfish? You want to talk about being selfish? You're the reason no one in Rowan County has any toilet paper!

EVAN: Yeah Dad. It's like the Cottenelle commercial says – share a square bro.

RACHEL: You bought up every single roll of toilet paper the first mention of a virus, stashing it in your end-of-the-world apocalyptic stockpile. You are worse than you were during Y2K! We can't even park our cars in the garage! I wonder what our neighbors would think if they knew you were the one responsible for the whole toilet paper shortage. If I told them about how you are hoarding toilet paper, they would come after you.

WESLEY: You're right I shouldn't have even bothered with the toilet paper. You just yell at me for putting it on the dispenser incorrectly anyway! I can never do anything right. You should be grateful.

RACHEL: Well heck we been together for 20 years – I'd think you'd know by now the proper way to put the toilet paper on the dispenser. It's not that complicated!

EVAN: Yeah, Dad.

WESLEY: And I would think that after 20 years you'd have quit nagging me about it by now!

EVAN: Yeah, Mom.

WESLEY: And I am not the only one who bought toilet paper in the neighborhood! You're just jealous that I was the one smart enough to stock up and it wasn't you.

[*There is angry silence between them, EVAN, unphased chuckles at something on his phone, then WESLEY looks out a window and draws in a deep breath as he points out the window*]

WESLEY: Look at those people out there in the park! They are not six feet apart!

RACHEL: OMG! You are not the Corona police! You are making me crazy, Wesley.

WESLEY: You were already that way when I met you. I am just keeping you safe.

RACHEL: O-M-G! I can't believe I am going to be stuck in this house with you for who knows how long!

EVAN [*laughing*]: Check out this Coronavirus meme!

[*EVAN shows his phone to his parents but they ignore him*]

WESLEY: You don't understand the seriousness of this. It hasn't even peaked yet! We could all die! And if we don't, the economy is going to crash!

RACHEL: It's all just a hoax.

WESLEY: No it's not! This marriage is a hoax, that's what's a hoax!

[*EVAN puts his hand up to his mouth*]

QUARREL-TINE | Connie Dinkler

WESLEY: You just touched your face, Evan.

[EVAN *calmly gets up and exits stage right, we hear water running and hear* EVAN *singing the happy birthday song*]

[RACHEL *stands up*]

EVAN [*offstage*]: Happy birthday to me.

Happy birthday to me.

Happy birthday dear Evan.
Happy birthday to me.

Happy birthday to me.

Happy birthday to me.

Happy birthday dear Evan.
Happy birthday to me.

RACHEL: That's it, I'm leaving.

WESLEY: Where are you going?

RACHEL: I need a drink.

WESLEY: Uh, the bars closed.

RACHEL: What!?

WESLEY [*matter-of-factly*]: I guess Governor Cooper doesn't consider them nearly as essential as you do.

RACHEL: Oh, if he had to live with you he would realize that the bars are definitely essential.

WESLEY: Maybe now is a good time for you to quit drinking.

[EVAN *enters stage right and sits back down in the same chair*]

RACHEL: No, no, no. This is the perfect time to increase my drinking.

[RACHEL *puts her hand on her forehead*]

WESLEY: You touched your face, Rachel. You really need to wash your hands.

EVAN: And don't forget the happy bir –

RACHEL [*angrily*]: I am not washing my hands again! I am not singing happy birthday to myself! And I am not wearing a stupid monogrammed face mask!

WESLEY: Well, you could at least use the hand sanitizer –

RACHEL: No! I am going to go to Mom and Dad's! [RACHEL *picks up her purse*] Evan, are you coming with me?

EVAN: I can Mom, but then how would I get my work done for school? Grandma and Grandpa's Internet is so slow it would be faster to mail my teachers letters.

RACHEL: Fine. Stay here with your father. But I am taking all the toilet paper with me!

[RACHEL *exits stage left. There is a pause, we hear a door slam.* WESLEY *sighs, leans back and places his hands on his forehead and smooths out his hair*]

EVAN: You just touched your face, Dad.

WESLEY: I know.

EVAN [*confused*]: You're not going to wash your hands?

WESLEY: Nah.

EVAN: But what about the Coronavirus?

WESLEY: Oh, I'm not too worried about it. It's probably just a marketing scheme created by the hand-sanitizer manufacturers. But I knew if I kept it up long enough your mother would get so angry she would go quarantine herself at your grandparents.

THE END

Quarrel-tine

WESLEY: Esta bien, lo siento.

RACHEL: ¿Por que siempre yo tengo que ir a hacer las compras?

[WESLEY *limpia las patas de la mesa*]

WESLEY: Por que siempre que yo lo hago, te quejas que no traje lo correcto.

RACHEL: ¡Es porque no traes lo correcto! Lo escribo todo detallado para ti! Ni siquiera un idiota podría de alguna manera equivocarse, pero tu siempre te equivocas.

WESLEY: ¡Tu eres muy exigente!

RACHEL: Tal vez no soy tan exigente, porque me casé contigo. ¿O no? Lo que pasa que eres muy flojo para tomarte el tiempo de leer la lista. ¿Que has hecho mientras yo estaba haciendo las diligencias? Evan, no seas como tu padre cuando te cases y dejes que tu esposa lo haga todo.

EVAN: Esta bien mamá.

WESLEY: He estado desinfectando la casa-

RACHEL: ¿Otra vez?

WESLEY: Y estaba viendo unas noticias especiales. El gobernador a puesto una orden de quedarse en casa en Carolina del Norte.

RACHEL [*sarcásticamente*]: ¡Oh! eso es maravilloso.

WESLEY: Por ahora no debemos salir de la casa excepto para ir a la farmacia o para comprar comida. Todos los negocios están cerrando excepto los esenciales.

RACHEL: ¿Entonces no podré tener mi mani-pedi?

WESLEY: No.

RACHEL: O ir a la cama de bronceado?

WESLEY: No.

RACHEL: ¿No puedo ir a las películas, o a cenar con mis amigas?

WESLEY: No.

RACHEL: ¿Que fregados puedo hacer entonces? ¡Ni siquiera puedo ir al trabajo! por lo menos podría alejarme.

WESLEY: Todavía puedes ir a la tienda a comprar lo que necesitas para cocinarnos la cena.

EVAN: Si, mamá

RACHEL [*sarcásticamente*]: ¡Oh! eso es divertido.

WESLEY: Rachel, no estaría tan mal. [*WESLEY busca debajo de la mesa y saca unas mascarillas*] !Mira! ¡Nos hice unas mascarillas con monogramas que coinciden!

RACHEL: ¿En serio?

WESLEY: Hice una para Fido también.

RACHEL: ¿Le hiciste una mascarilla con monograma al perro?

WESLEY: Si. Pero pienso que tengo que ajustarla, no estaba seguro como hacer las tiras que van sobre sus orejas, estoy trabajando en eso.

RACHEL: Me estas matando.

WESLEY: No, pero Covid-19 te matara si no usas una de estas.

[*RACHEL pone su mano en su frente y suspira*]

WESLEY: Tocaste tu cara, Rachel.

RACHEL: Que?

WESLEY: Has tocado tu cara. Ahora tienes que lavarte las manos.

RACHEL: ¡Apenas me lave las manos cuando vine! ¡No necesito lavármelas otra vez!

WESLEY: No importa, debes levarte las manos. No deberías tocarte la cara Rachel. ¡Dicen COVID-19 puede vivir asta tres días en superficies!

RACHEL [*muy enojada*]: ¡Dijiste que apenas desinfectases la casa!

WESLEY: Si pero no lo eh terminado todo.

RACHEL: ¡Oh Dios mío! ¡No puedes estar aquí con tu hipocondría las veinticuatro horas del día!

WESLEY: Lo siento querida. Creo que soy un poco sobre protectivo. Recuerda que estamos en esto juntos. [*WESLEY comienza a rociar el sofá con desinfectante*] ¿No te vas a probar la mascara?

RACHEL: ¡Yo no me voy a poner eso! ¡Me va a arruinar el maquillaje! ¿Sabes cuanto tiempo me lleva para maquillarme?

WESLEY: Absolutamente lo se. ¿Estas realmente preocupada por tu maquillaje cuando hay personas muriendo?

RACHEL [*frenéticamente*]: ¡Muriendo – eso me recuerda! [*RACHEL recorre sus dedos entre su cabello*] Me tengo que hacer las raíces pronto! ¿Que voy a hacer?

EVAN: Te tocaste la cara otra ves, mamá.

RACHEL: Evan, estas castigado.

Tiny Frozen Doilies Falling from the Sky

Selma Dragoș

Cast

ADRIANA BLĂJAN/ADRIANA PRESECANU/ARIEL: a fortyish woman transported by panic attacks from one universe to the another.

At Rise

A supermarket. At the crossroads between the meat, seafood, and deli, a woman is having a panic attack.

It's cold. Didn't I have a jacket on? It's so cold. I suddenly find myself falling down a long deep hollow. A dried salami, a few bologna slices and two smoked hams look worriedly over the edge of the pit. A sodium nitrate-filled pâté teddy bear stares into my eyes and asks "Are you all right?". Even his voice sounds synthetic! [*Imitates a toy voice*] "Are you okay? Beep! Beep!" [*Chokes*] I can't laugh as I gasp for air. I breathe it in and in but can't breathe it out. I fill up like a balloon, but I keep falling. What the fuck? I gasp for more air. Still heavy. Still falling. The air's itself is thick and heavy, that's why I am not rising. Fucking hell, that's just my luck – if a pit is going to open at my feet, then it must be in the coldest place on earth, at the crossroads of frozen foods, deli, and seafood aisles. The big fish at the top of the counter stares at me with a gaping mouth and empty eyes. Just like me, he knows his fall is going to end with a thud on a cold surface.

I take a deeper breath, I try to self-inflate and fly away.

The air's getting thicker. Turns into water. Then soup. Thick soup. Jelly. Ice.

I'm left with my mouth agape, a frozen fossil waiting to be freed by global warming.

"Knock! Knock! Do you want me to call someone?" asks the pâté teddy, smiling encouragingly.

I can't answer as I gasp for air. The teddy bear smiles back and lands his paw on my shoulder. His warm clawy grasp feels like an embrace. I thaw, deflate and collapse next to my shopping cart.

"Are you all right?" asks [*reads her name tag*] Mrs. Ancuța HereForYou, the frozen foods aisle manager . So young and already managing things! I wonder whether Mr. HereForYou is proud of her. Or is he the type who's jealous of his wife's success?

[...]

[*A room at the back of a supermarket*]

I wouldn't have thought supermarkets had rooms to hide fallen people. So this stuff does happen. Falling women. Maybe men fall too. And children.

"Onuța! Onuțaaaaa?! Onuța? Where's Onuța?"

This must be where Ancuța HereForYou and her sister (or is she more of a distant cousin?), Mariana HereForYou, hide the fallen. So as not to scare the customers. And prevent contagion. It would be very unpleasant for the HereForYous if customers started falling down abysses between the shelves by the dozens.

"My Onuța. Where's Onuța?"

"Who's Onuța?" asks Mrs. Customer Relations Mădălina HereForYou.

What do you know! It's a family business, this supermarket. Wow.

"Onuța is my little girl. I lost her. She was in the little red car attached to the shopping cart!"

I am screaming.

"Where's Onuța? My little girl! Where's my little girl?"

Ancuța makes an in-store announcement that a little girl is missing, four years old, orange overalls, red cap.

"She was riding the red car attached to the shopping cart!"

"Shh," says Mădălina HereForYou, "you had a regular shopping cart, no red car attached. Your shopping cart is here."

"That's not mine! Mine had a little red car attached! I had bought: Nesquik cereal, milk, feta cheese, cottage cheese, red onions, potatoes, carp roe caviar, Romanian apples, margarine,

"Authentic Romanian Taste" corn puffs, teddy bear-shaped pork pâté ..."

"But the coat and wallet in this cart are obviously yours, miss ... Ariel ... ma'am ..."

"That is not the cart I was shopping with."

"Look, the coat is yours, we found your ID in its pocket ... and your license ... So your surname is Blăjan? Adrianaa, ah, obviously. Ariel is just a stage name ... yes, obviously ..."

I don't listen to her anymore... I run out of the room and find myself in a colorless hallway. Huge metal doors at both ends. No doorknobs. I run to the right, push the gate. Backyard. Opposite direction. It's closed. I push. I punch.

"Onuța!"

Onu'a throws a horrible tantrum even when I lock myself in the bathroom for five minutes. Afraid to be alone, she says. Actually, she senses how I long to sneak out the window, climb down the fire escape and make a run for it. That's why she never leaves my side. Children sense these things. Her anxiety and tantrums are all expressions of my own despair. Fucking fuck! Being lost in a supermarket is going to leave her scarred for life! I run across the yard. There is a fence. I climb. My jeans get caught right where they were already ripped.

[*Beat. One confused moment*]

Didn't I upcycle these jeans a long time ago? I made a chic diaper bag out of them ...

[*Beat*]

I land on my feet on the other side. Land on my feet! Me! I never land on my feet! [*Beat*] And I haven't worn sneakers since I was 28. What's all with all these horrible sequins? [*Beat*]

"Onuța!"

I run back to the front, push the revolving front door, shout "sorry" over my shoulder to the woman who curses at me. I run to the guard. He puts his hand on my arm and speaks into his walkie talkie:

"Found her!"

[*Back room again*]

I scan the shopping cart: prosecco, peaches, strawberries, two of those big individually packed expensive avocados, a pineapple, nuts, cashews, pistachios, and fish. The one with the gaping mouth and anguished look in its eyes ... Where's my teddy bear-shaped pâté?

"Stop calling me Ariel. I don't know who Ariel is! I'm Adriana Presecanu."

"You're Adriana Blăjan, it says so on your ID."

What's wrong with these people?! I breathe in. I breathe out. In two–three–four. Out two–three–four–five–six. I use my most soothing tone:

"Blăjan is my maiden name, Presecanu is my husband's surname and I took it as well after our marriage. Sergiu Presecanu, I'll give you his phone number. Our little girl, Onuța Presecanu, orange jumpsuit, red cap, blonde, brown eyes, was with me. We were shopping. She was riding the little red car attached to the shopping cart. She got lost. Why are you not looking for her?!!!"

Mr. Guardian Horațiu HereForYou tells me to calm down.

Mrs. Customer Relations Mădălina HereForYou addresses me as "Miss Blăjan" and "Ariel."

"Ariel" was my stage name in college, when Sergiu and I were in a band together. He gave me that stage name. He said it was cool, that it made you think of the Disney mermaid but it was also a bit ... mysterious, androgynous. Onuța! Where's Onuța?

"Onuța! Did you find her? I'll sue you! She could be ... someone could be ... who knows what could happen while you're holding me here!"

"Calm down, Miss Blăjan."

A siren. An ambulance. Onuța!

"The ambulance came for my daughter, didn't it?! Why won't you tell me ... what happened ... to her."

Ouch!...

[*Slaps her arm as if an insect bites her*]

[...]

[*An ambulance.*]

In the ambulance a muscular blond man strokes my hand, gently.

"Onuța? Where's Onuța?"

"You had a seizure ... a seizure ..." says the big blond. "You'll be fine. You'll see, in two hours you'll be signing autographs ..."

TINY FROZEN DOILIES FALLING FROM THE SKY | *Selma Dragoș*

I fall asleep. I dream I'm signing autographs with a black marker on slippery butcher paper. Mothers stand in line, flashes flash, a famous journalist interviews me. I multitask, as always.

"Live from the shelf where the incident occurred, the unwitting mother who abandoned her little girl at the crossroads of meat, deli, and seafood reveals firsthand information." She turns to me smiling thinly, "Ma'am, you allowed yourself an anxiety attack in broad daylight, in front of your daughter, thus neglecting the emotional well-being of a child. How could you?!"

"Oh, I indulged," I reply "I often do."

The crowd of mothers roars in disbelief.

[...]

The therapist believes that I, Ariel, had this burn out, this breakdown, this checking out of my own self because of the midlife crisis. As it were, my biological clock was ticking and I realized I was never going to have children. And that realization was a huge shock to my psyche.

She says: "Psychological decompensation. Your psyche split. It created false memories of another life where you were a married woman, mother of two daughters."

My psyche should be a total moron to prefer to be a wife and mother whose every minute belongs to someone else to the life of luxury and freedom of a pop star! I don't say it out loud, though. No more talk of alternate dimensions, portals, parallel lives, being another version of myself, either. It took me two weeks to believe it myself.

I say what they expect to hear.

"It was a moment of weakness, caused by sadness and burnout. But now, after two weeks of rest and therapy, I realize it could have ended badly. I was overworked and sleep deprived."

"This could be the title of the album I'm working on," I say. "Burn out. Break down. Check-out."

Ardere. Rupere. Ieșire. Sounds better in Romanian, for once.

The "girls" in the group are enrapt in my words. Yeah, of course I'll invite them to the album release! Oh, yeah, right. We'll go out for drinks afterwards. Ups, no drinks! Tea! And afterwards, touched by fame and glamor, they'll accidentally drop my name in conversations with colleagues and friends,

Selma Dragoș | TINY FROZEN DOILIES FALLING FROM THE SKY

I give them autographs on the rehab center brochure. For the daughters at home. I do it like I practiced on all my notebooks in high school. Something tells me that if I've become a pop star and my name is Ariel, that's how I sign my name.

I make a commitment to start living like a sensible woman, eat, pray, love, and accept the inevitable degradation of my body, mind and sex appeal. We're talking like 40-something women in a support group, because that is what we are. I'm careful not to stir their envy. I'm careful to give the impression that I'm not happy to be who I am. I subtly imply that I even envy them a little for their barbecue-scented husbands and their spoiled brats. I refrain from screaming in their faces:

"Been there, got rid of that. Not sorry for a second! I'm free, you stupid bitches! Run, bitches, run!"

But I don't want to give the therapist an excuse to keep me in here any longer. So I say:

"I was so wrong, this is not the life one should be living at my age. I have a responsibility to myself and to the young girls who are my fans. It's unrealistic to look the way I look. Clearly there's a price. A hidden cost. I am not buying into that fantasy any longer." My feigned "growth" reassures everyone enough.

In the end, we all have to get back to our lives.

[...]

Every morning, over coffee, I repeat this myself, to stay sane:

"This is the truth. I used to be Adriana Presecanu. A music teacher at secondary school. I used to have a four-year-old daughter – Onuța. And a teenage daughter – Adina. I was married to Sergiu Presecanu, the former bass player of our college band. He had become a sales agent for a plumbing company.

He was cheating on me. With a singer my age. I was scanning old photos from our youth, and when I uploaded them, I found a video of her in the cloud. She was stripping to his playing on a guitar. I grabbed our younger daughter and ran away from home. To a supermarket. Where else would I run? I had a panic attack and slipped into a pa–ra–llel–u–ni–verse."

Since I switched universes, I speak freely of reincarnation, parallel dimensions and such and I have no problem saying things like "fuck you like hurricane". I swear a lot, never keep stuff in to spare anyone's feelings.

I repeat to myself: "I'm Adriana Blăjan, I believe in parallel universes, the horoscope and soulmates – why not? I mean, if all this was possible, why not? – I've never been married, no children, no obligations. My stage name is Ariel. I look 28. And I'm a star."

For a while I was still confusing people and worlds. So I made a list:

Gențiana is my manager. She's the most important presence in my life. We call three times a day.

Mom's still Mom. We see each other at Christmas and Easter. Sometimes she calls to guilt trip me for not calling. We have nothing else to talk about, really.

Dad's still Dad. Same as with Mom. Minus the guilt trips.

Melinda's still my sister. We talk on the phone every week. We pretend to like each other in this dimension as well. She lives on the same block as my mother.

Sergiu Presecanu, my husband-in-another-dimension – is a salesman for a plumbing company. Here – I Googled him – he's the director of an advertising agency. Apparently, I've made a few videos for his agency, but we don't seem to have any personal relationship. Good riddance. His wife is the daughter of the agency owner. He has two children: Adriana – did he name her after me? And Adam.

This is my place. I own an apartment, in this universe. I am quite well off, it seems – from the clothes and perfumes and stuff I have. It is not big, but it's uptown, so ...

To think that therapist is holding on to the theory that my psyche would prefer to be a working mother and wife. I have a very hard time keeping a straight face during our weekly sessions where we talk about how maybe it's not too late for me and my uterus to join the ranks of the blessed.

Not that I'm not working. I am just working for myself, on myself. When I am not working, I am working out.

If I open the couch, there's no room to exercise. To do my live fitness stream in the morning, I move the couch into the kitchen, bring the flower pot from the hallway and push everything aside. It's all in the angle of the camera. I have this account, on a site, and upload fitness routines. Sometimes people get a bit intense. I only do fitness routines, though.

[...]

[*A brightly lit stage, instruments, projections, music. A slow, sentimental song Ariel/Adriana is miming singing into the microphone, alternating the mimed song with speaking to the audience*]

I look into the crowd. They're all so young. They adore me.

I could be their mother. None of them think about it. Not one of them thinks their mothers are my age.

But I do. And I feel like a winner.

A crunchy, dark-haired soft-skinned boy comes up to me for an autograph and doesn't leave my side for hours. His eyes twinkle. He stares at me but what he sees is not me. He sees everything anyone could want. He sees the guarantee that you can have the world. If a woman can have the world at her feet and a man can fuck her, that makes one master of the world. If one brings her to her knees, one has brought the world to its knees. We fuck under a crystal chandelier in the bathroom of an expensive hotel.

I am not sure this should be called fucking. It's feels more like a choreography. I recognize this choreography from one of the videos Sergiu made with his mistress. How come they both want to make the exact same moves in the exact same order? Even "You like it, say you like it, you little bitch." Same words, same intonation. How can two men, in two separate dimensions, have such similar fantasies? And then it dawns on me, as I pretend to orgasm: "It's the porn!" And I stop pretending, right in the middle of it.

I wonder how many other women validated this with their fake moans and giggles.

Maybe I'll use this take in my goodnight text to the mysterious Prospero2020. I'll say something like "during the last month i had sex with 4 different guys and they all seemed to want the same positions in the same order, what's up with that?". Of course, I won't mention the parallel universe part. There is a possibility that he is a journalist or something.

The crunchy boy is now strutting like a rooster, feeling like a winner. He'll be telling his friends about this for years. I don't know

TINY FROZEN DOILIES FALLING FROM THE SKY | *Selma Dragoș*

why, I just can't let him have his victory. I go, "So, you call this ... what we just had ... sex?" The ancient statue melts down with uncertainty, like gingerbread soaked in milk. He runs out just in time to avoid breaking in two.

In this universe, I'm the man.

This is how I end my text to Prospero2020, after detailing the whole experience to him. "I am the man."

He writes, deletes, writes, deletes. Then says, "You should write a song with that title. But make it grunge."

We have only been chatting for a week now, but he gets me so well.

I'll go back to the grunge I used to make with Sergiu, in college. That was more me. I find it very hard to enjoy my own concerts sometimes. What experiences shaped me in this universe, how did I come to be all romance and sweetness? Or am I lying? For the brand?

[...]

[*In the same apartment, a few months later, in the evening*]

I walk around the house naked and pretend to forget I don't have curtains. I feel the eyes of the neighbor across the street. I sit at the window. How close these blocks are. Her husband's back is turned. At some point, always at some point, he follows her gaze. And they both look at me. Naked. He quickly turns his back. I can feel his Adam's apple rolling. Then she gets angry and closes the curtains. She wants to slam them, but they're cloth. I know for sure I'm ruining her evening. Every night. And she's even younger than me.

What's Sergiu in this universe? I'd like Sergiu to see me as I am now. He wouldn't want us to "divorce without a fuss, for the sake of the children."

[...]

Scroll.

Scroll.

Click. Scroll.

"Incendiary! Find out which star is selling nude photos online".

Shit.

It could be anyone.

Click. Scroll.

Gentiana looks at me reproachfully.

Click. Scroll.

Gentiana says: "I asked you if there was anything ..."

Photos and screenshots are taken by a subscriber. Some journalist. It was a matter of time, anyway. You can't see the face. But Gentiana knows it's me.

Gentiana says: "You should've told me, to do damage control ... if you really didn't have enough money ..."

"What damage, Gentiana?" I shout. "There's no damage. It's 2020! You didn't want me to start crocheting bags and doilies to pay for all this, did you?! I wouldn't even have time to crochet. Anyway, you can't see your face. It could be anyone. They're bluffing, there will be no follow up."

[...]

Prospero2020 says "You're a goddess."

"Which one?" I ask him.

"All of them." he says.

I give in and send him my personal number. We get off the site but keep on texting. I love the mystery and I love that he never asks for photos or videos. He just likes to text.

"Under what name should I save you?" I ask him.

"Call me by any name you like" he says. And I don't insist.

Sometimes we chat all night. There's something between us, a spark, something alive. I work out, starve myself, dance and do vocals all day with him in mind.

I ask him why we don't meet face to face. He laughs.

"Are you playing with fire, goddess? Wanna start over?"

I don't get it. So there was something between us? Were the shredded shirts I found in the apartment his shirts?

I venture to ask, "Remind me, what did we fight about?"

He says, "That's why I love you. Give me some time."

I ask "Have you forgiven me?"

Writes, erases, writes, erases. Answers "I love you."

He sends me a huge bouquet of lilacs via courier. That's when I know he's my soulmate. I know it's for real because it's so spiritual: I have no idea how he looks like, or how he sounds like, but our minds have fucked each other silly for months now, via text and sometimes the occasional whispered voice call.

TINY FROZEN DOILIES FALLING FROM THE SKY | *Selma Dragoş*

He says it's sexier this way. I agree. With all the recordings and photos of myself. This minimalism makes it feel special.

[...]

Click. Scroll. Scroll. Shit. Fuzz dot com. Bozo dot net. Home page of most news sites.

Click. Scroll. There's also a video of me naked, languidly calling out to someone who can't be seen. Calling him my Prospero. It's recent and it's filmed in my apartment.

I stare in disbelief.

Then I hear his voice off camera and freeze. How did I not know it's Sergiu?

Gentiana is yelling at me.

Inhale, exhale.

My teeth are chattering with sudden cold. I clench my trembling fists and push the words out: "Gentiana, darling, it would be worth the drama if I looked like a cheap ball that spent all summer in the sun. It would be dramatic if I were a failed music teacher looking at the pictures from my youth and the hairy, chubby idiot I'd been married to would sigh and say he'd been duped with false advertising."

My own words make me hot again. I stop shivering. I go on.

"I am free woman, I am going to own this, Gentiana. Own my body and my gorgeous tits and my perfectly shaved cunt. It's truly nobody else's business how I choose to use them."

Gentiana screams again.

Her agency can't afford this stuff ... sponsoring events for kids. We're over.

As I exit her office, I take a step back to see myself in the mirror. In this universe I have the perfect poker face. You wouldn't know it hurts.

I get hate on Facebook. Carnage in the mom groups.

Eh, I figured. You can always count on mommy groups to tear you down, especially when you're already the target of public ridicule. Every few hours one of them says, "Well, with all the surgery and care you have to put in to look like that at 40, they're obviously all prostituting themselves! No children, no obligations, all day in the gym, massages, cosmetics. She couldn't live like that on honest work!"

No, actually, I could not.

"Whore."

[...]

I had the number blocked. Once I knew to look, the messages, and the pictures, everything came flooding back. He was blocked on Facebook, everywhere. Sergiu. It had been him all along.

Sergiu is my karma in all universes. I call him, he hangs up on me. I write to Prospero2020: "Sergiu! Why?" He answers late, full of apologies. "I couldn't. I told the crazy woman I was getting a divorce and she went through my phone. She sent the video to cancan dot ro."

I write: " You mother fucker I hope your dicks breaks in your mom's ass."

Hours of beeping.

Beep. "It's not my fault! The bitch is crazy and vengeful. I can't do it without you." Beep. "I'm going crazy without you." Beep. "Every cell in me is screaming for you." "You know you can't live without me, either!"

[*Hums "Every cell in me is screaming for you"*] Huh! that's the type of cheesy thing I sell, it's only fair I get it back.

Beep "Forgive me." Beep. "I need to see you." Beep "You don't understand what I'm going through here. Adriana, you're gonna be sorry." Beep "Let's stop hurting each other." Beep. "Come on, my little panther, we'll laugh about this one day." Beep "I'm downstairs." Beep "Adriana, without you nothing has life. Neither do I. Please don't make me…" Beep "Adriana, you'll regret it if you let pride kill the heart."

Wow. "Don't let pride kill the heart!" Instant top ten hit.

Beep "You changed the code!???? What the fuck do you take me for? What did you think, girl? That I'd come over uninvited? Or did you give it to others as well? You dirty whore. Go swallow more pills, then. See If I care."

Oh! Aaaah! So in this dimension, that's how I ended up in the hospital.

Turn out I am not that clever here either.

Ring. "It's raining. It's cold. Like my soul since we last spoke. Open up."

Ahahaha. It's raining in his soul. Sergiu. It's raining in his soul.

TINY FROZEN DOILIES FALLING FROM THE SKY | Selma Dragoş

"I love you."

Of all the possible futures, in all the possible dimensions, in all the universe, I walk into one in which I am Sergiu's mistress.

Knock–knock. Someone must have opened the door downstairs for him. He whispers to me through the keyhole. "I missed you like a cut-off limb."

I choke with laughter. The lines my Sergiu has got in this universe! Like the ones he used to send his mistress in the other universe. Oh, wait. I *am* the mistress. He's cleaned up nicely in this one. He's got white teeth, perfect implants. Same hairy belly, though.

I win.

"I'm sorry, you got me too excited," says Sergiu. "This happens. No big deal. Why are you laughing?"

"Tell me," I ask, "what do I see in you? Why am I your mistress? Surely I can do better," I say, pointing at our reflections in the mirror above the bed.

"You don't see it," he says, "but you feel it. We both know. We're soul mates."

Fuck me. He really is my soul mate. Holy sister! Fuck. Twenty–twenty.

I lived for 40 years twice, in two separate universes. In one of them I raised two kids, taught piano in middle school, and went on only two vacations in 20 years – with the kids. In the other, I trained every day for 20 years, worked on my voice every day, starved myself, ended up singing syrupy songs, because they sell, waved my buttocks on stage and anonymously on the internet, because they sell too. There are probably millions parallel universes and in all of them my reward is ... SERGIU!

I push him and lock him out on the balcony. I throw his clothes out the window. The clothes fly off and land in the tree in front of the building. I dive in this daytime soap without any embarrassment that the neighbors are watching. The one across pulls the curtains wide. She is enjoying this. Let all the women on all the floors rejoice. I turn on my speakers and microphone, and plug in my guitar. I turn up the volume and sing:

"Haha, how unhappy

"She has become

"Haha, how she's lost

Selma Dragoș | TINY FROZEN DOILIES FALLING FROM THE SKY

"Haha, how she was betrayed.
"On the first floor
"Woman is crying
"On the second floor
"Woman's heart breaks
"On the third floor
"Woman falls on her knees
"On the fourth floor
"Woman gets back on her feet.
"Fifth
"Woman jumps.
"On the ground floor the sisters gossip
"Blood splashed on their crochet.
"Haha, how unhappy
"She has become
"Haha, how she's lost
"Hahahaha, how she was betrayed."

Sergiu is banging his fists on the window. Good, that should keep him warm. Snowflakes start falling while I scream. Sirens can't silence me, but the metal door finally gives way. Firemen come through the window, police come through the door. They are all here to rescue the man. To restore peace to the neighborhood. They unplug me, disconnect me, but can't take my microphone away. I howl into it as I faint.

[...]

[*Supermarket clerk*]

"You're better" says Mădălina Hereforyou as she hands me a cotton swab to hold over the puncture. She says they've found Onuța.

Onuța who?

Your daughter.

"Mrs. Presecan," says the doctor is here for you, "please, let's not do *that* again!"

Good. I'm back in the universe I left. Or some other similar place. Okay. It's clear to me there's no point in explaining myself. The little Onuța had stuck to the wafer stand, and didn't even notice I was gone. I found her pleading with someone in a cow suit for a third wafer. I pick her up, leave the cart right there.

TINY FROZEN DOILIES FALLING FROM THE SKY | Selma Dragoş

[...]
The video of me singing on the way to the ambulance has gone viral.
Even feminists like me now. Even the moms in mommy groups love me. My sisters love me now, and I love them. As if we were never enemies. I'm invited to talk about the burden of eternal youth. About the burden of the womb that needs to be used. About the burden of the love narrative that movies and pop music feed us.
I tell them how Gentiana said that no one would buy an album about the "Frozen goods aisle" and that I should get those facials more often, because I can't afford to sag.
I tell them that women like Gentiana prefer to think that if the world isn't theirs, they're to blame, that they don't eat yogurt and don't do enough core and glutes exercises.
I sing, I talk about the other life, then about this one. I tell the whole truth and nothing but the truth – except for Gentiana's name, in reality they don't call her that. In reality I've never had an agent, because I can't afford it, I manage myself. Otherwise, it's all true. I sing some more, then I make up a fictional ending for my other life:
Sergiu's not answering his phone. I text him "I'm okay with the divorce. See you in court."
He calls me right back. I don't answer.
Beep "Adriana, I made a huge mistake. Forgive me, my love."
I throw the phone out the window. I go into the bedroom, open the spotless wardrobe and take out all his shirts one by one – such shame I ironed them yesterday!
The bushes in front of the windows go gray, blue, and white. They clean up good with ties, trousers, shirts – makes them look more masculine, more poised. They look like dependable family bushes now.
My daughters Adina and Onuța laugh with me as we throw more things out the window. Adina looks at me in admiration for the first time in years.
"Well done, Mummy, it was about time," she says.
I take out my guitar and start
"Sisters, dear sisters,
"Sharpen your knives

"Cut out your hearts
"Throw them away
"And fill your chests with ice."
Someone's turning a key in the lock.
It's Sergiu.
I block the door from the inside.
Knock–knock. Excuse me, do you have time to talk about soul mates?
Onuța shouts "We're not home!". Through the peephole Sergiu looks like a fish with a gaping mouth and an anguished look. A fish frozen in another era.
It's snowing.
Tiny ice doillies are falling from the sky.
It's snowing so beautifully, it makes you want to open your mouth wide.
To swallow the world whole, flakes and all.
Billions of tiny unique doilies are falling and falling.
Some disintegrate when they touch the ground, some break each others' fall.
It's snowing.
I hold my daughters in my arms.
It's nice and warm.

THE END

Mileuri mici de gheaţă

Video-ul cu mine cântând în drum spre ambulanță a devenit viral.
Chiar și feministele mă plac acum. Mămicile de pe grupurile de mămici mă adoră. Sunt invitată să vorbesc despre povara tinereții veșnice. Despre povara uterului care trebuie folosit. Despre povara narațiunii despre iubire cu care ne îndoapă filmele și muzica pop.
Le povestesc cum Gențiana zicea că nimeni n-ar cumpăra un album despre „raionul congelate" și că ar fi cazul să fac mai des tratamentele alea faciale, că nu-mi permit să mă fleșcăiesc.

TINY FROZEN DOILIES FALLING FROM THE SKY | Selma Dragoș

Le spun că femei ca Gențiana preferă să creadă că, dacă lumea nu e a lor, ele-s de vină, că nu papă iaurțelul și nu fac destule exerciții pentru fesieri.

Cânt, vorbesc despre viața cealaltă, apoi despre cea de acum. Spun tot adevărul și numai adevărul – mai puțin numele Gențianei, în realitate nu o cheamă așa. În realitate n-am avut niciodată agent, că nu-mi permit, îmi fac singură managementul. În rest, e adevărat tot. Mai cânt, pe urmă bag un final fictiv pentru cealaltă viață.

[...]

Fiicele mele, Adina și Onuța râd cu mine în timp ce aruncăm lucruri pe geam.

Onuța râde.

Adina se uită pentru prima dată cu admirație la mine.

„Bravo, mami, era și timpul", zice.

Iau chitara și încep

"La toate etajele
Plânge doar femeile
La toate etajele
Se sfâșie inimele
La toate etajele
Se bârfesc vecinele.
La toate etajele
Plânge doar femeile.
La toate etajele
Își zgârie pleoapele
La toate etajele
Eu îmi văd surorile.
La toate etajele
Mamele și fiicele
Își ascut cuțitele
Să-și scoată inimile
Să le-arunce peste bloc
Să își pună gheață-n loc
La toate etajele
Câștigă femeile. "

Adina mi-a moștenit vocea. Onuța dansează pe pat. Ușa e blocată bine, am deconectat interfonul.

Cineva încearcă cheia, e Sergiu.
Cioc-cioc. Primiți cu sufletul pereche? Bate deja cu pumnul.
Mă uit la fiică-mea, îmi face cu ochiul. „Nu suntem acasă, mama."
Chicotim. Onuța strigă „Nu suntem acasăăăăă!"
Pe vizor, prin ușa dublă, Sergiu arată ca un pește cu cap mare, umflat și ochi sticloși, de creatură care cade. Un pește înghețat în altă eră.
Ninge.
Mileuri mici de gheață cad din cer
Ninge așa frumos, că-ți vine să deschizi gura mare
Să înghiți lumea întreagă cu fulgi cu tot.
Ninge mileuri irepetabile din cer.
Cad și cad.
Unele se topesc la fel când ating pământul. Altele cad în brațele surorilor deja căzute.
Ninge.
Îmi strâng fiicele în brațe.
E cald și bine.

Two Lovers and a Bear: An Occult Romantic Comedy About Soul Mates and the Roles We Play

Tjaša Ferme

Cast

MALINA, Princess Aquamarine: a complex young woman, she thinks she knows what she wants. She constantly and suddenly changes her opinions and moods; she thrives on drama. She is comical because she takes herself so seriously

KARST, Prince Proteus: patient and a philosophically inspired young man, which doesn't mean that he is not practical. It is comical how seriously he takes MALINA

BEAR: a tall man, dressed up as a bear. He looks dignified and even handsome, but he is not for jokes

VOICE: behind the door

Time

Now.

Setting

At some moment in the play the characters on stage realize that every scene has a different lighting design. These lighting changes may be reminiscent of Instagram filters, but it is up to the design team. Perhaps this play explains soul mates and soul groups, but don't we all just play roles, anyways?

Scene 1

[*Spotlight on a bed*]

MALINA: Do you know when I realized that this is something special?

In Macedonia! Because I was so happy every time I saw you. Because you were so intensely present and we lingered over breakfast for so long that it was suddenly lunchtime.

The fact I love you and I could even fall in love with you is less indicative that we should be together than the fact that I can stand you. And that you make me happy every time just by looking at you.

It is true that I am a tad stubborn and inflexible, but you are flexible. Yet you have the integrity to quickly put me in my place when I am out of line. I like that.

It's easier to consider all these options if I pretend my life is fiction.
[*She says everything, even some of the stage directions, except if in italics. She is the creator of reality as well as the actress in it*]

Scenario 1

MALINA: Your face completely brightens up, you kiss me and that's it. I smile.

[KARST *kisses her.* MALINA: *In affected language with no regional specialties. Bravo. You brilliantly felt the moment when they kiss, like in a Hollywood movie. Because you're a movie director you instinctively felt what's the most appropriate*]

Scenario 2

MALINA: Your face lights up with a smile and in a sexy provocative way you ask me:

KARST: And in what case could you fall in love with me?

MALINA [*with a smile of a satisfied princess*]: If you swear that you'll love me, that you're mine and you'll do anything for me.

KARST: Aha, so does this oath require anything special? Like kneeling?

MALINA: Yes, of course, kneeling.

KARST: I swear I love you and I'd do anything for you, for you to be happy and fulfilled and ... do you think this is good?

MALINA: With a smile of a shyly satisfied princess, giggling out of the excitement, I sigh I do.

[*They kiss. Then they look at each other for a while and then laugh*]

MALINA: She is excitingly squealing like a Fairy Raspberry. [*"Vila Malina" for reference*]
KARST: He is laughing his strange belly laugh in even patterns with mini pauses; it is coming out of wonder and excitement as if he had just witnessed a daisy birthing a ladybug.
KARST: And now you're in love?
MALINA: I shrug.
[*MALINA erupts even though she wants to hold back; it isn't exactly easy to talk about this*]
MALINA: Once I was upset with you because you didn't protect me. When the Russian Sasha in Siberia wanted to fuck me, and I didn't want to fuck him, you just left me because you misread the signals. Or when the other Russian, also Sasha, went after me in Macedonia, you also withdrew, 'cause you didn't get that I wanted you! And that it's normal that everybody always wants to fuck me and that it's different for women. I won't just go with anyone that's into me. But I do know that if a woman is crazy about a man, it is necessary to accept. That pissed me off less because of these concrete examples and more because it testifies about your values.

Scenario 3

MALINA: You know if you reject me, we'll never see each other again? My ego couldn't take it.
KARST: Oh, come on. Why would I reject you?
MALINA: Because you never want to commit to anybody.
KARST: Well ... no.
MALINA: Maybe you became "the guy" in my imagination because you were the only man to ever live my version of the perfect life with me: travel with me, work on my projects with me, the man I can talk to about everything I'm interested in and go deep. Well, also a guy with whom I have seen a stuffed Siberian wolf and in front of whom I dared to be a bad girl. [*Aside*] Oops I slipped into a real cliché of contemporary American kitchen-sink drama, I look into the audience if this really is a show and I also say all the stage directions aloud [*back to KARST*] and I peed in front of you in a teapot. [*To herself*] Still pretty literary sounding [*back to KARST*] by that I took revenge for the poor hospitality

of a Moscow hotel. Or does "Russian hotel" sound better? [*Asks KARST*] I just realized that between every scenario there is a different Instagram light filter on stage. [*Looks at the TECHNICIAN in the booth*] Have you been doing that?

TECHNICIAN: Yup.

MALINA: By the way, I don't know if you noticed that I said "the guy" – not "the one" because I'm too aloof and insecure. I would never say that – "the one." Love confessions are risky. Because if you weren't feeling the same, you would be flattered, and if your freedom was more important to you, you would still say no. With a lot of kind apologizing, and even if I ever forgave you, I would never admit it, 'cause I would be too ashamed. That a man won again, that I admitted my love to someone, and he said, "No, thank you, but I'm really honored." Oh, again the pain: when you're ripped open in the middle and your guts spill out. You'd rather the flames swallow you alive than have anybody notice what just happened. One is, of course, most afraid of public humiliation. Please just don't post about it! Old wounds open up, old stitches break apart, and old scabs that have been slyly hiding underneath the surface of the skin, gush out, flooding the marinas, crushing bridges and demolishing dams.

[*This is expressed overtly poetically on purpose. Turns to the audience*]

MALINA: I *want* to give you diabetes.

KARST: Oh, I would never want to hurt you this much, please stop.

MALINA: And, you know who would play you on stage? Ethan Hawke – twenty years younger, of course – also one of the loves of my life, who got off the hamster wheel ...

KARST: "... got off the hamster wheel"? He had a great life, awesome career, ran away with the nanny ... if he's a hamster, I'm a hamster ...

MALINA: You actually look like that. [*KARST cannot help but to laugh*] I lay down seductively, oh, I'm really glad that you're playing this game with me now ...

[*They kiss*]

KARST: Yes.

[*They kiss again*]

MALINA: Want to have kids with me?

KARST: We could arrange something ...

MALINA: I'm a little bit worried they would be too pale-skinned, I always imagined I would have a mixed child. We look too much alike. But I think you'd make a great dad. I guess we'll just be making pasty babies then. I always dreamed of having a United Colors of Benetton family. Every child of different color. But I wouldn't birth them myself and I wouldn't serve them myself! I guess it was more an idea of children I wanted to hang out with as a child than having them. Little Berlin hipsters.

Our household will have to be really democratic – I can't do everything by myself!

I would like to live in some kind of a commune, but once we get together, I would like us to be in love for a while. I want to feel chosen, special for a while. Then we can discuss polyamory since I know that's what you're thinking. I'm also concerned about au pairs. For her to be too beautiful, too young, too French, and you'd have an affair with her.

Scenario 4

MALINA: But honestly does it make sense to have children now?

KARST: You mean because of the pandemic?

MALINA: I mean, because of the state of the world. With how dysfunctional our systems are ...

KARST: But it's always been this way.

MALINA: It has? What do you mean? I think we've never been so overpopulated and polluted.

KARST: We've had other problems in the past, but it always felt like bringing more humans on board is a bad idea and not safe.

[Beat]

MALINA: You know there's a corona baby boom, right?

KARST: I didn't notice.

MALINA: Yah, all my friends are having kids.

[Beat]

MALINA: But I wonder, you know ... I think we might go extinct in the next ten years or so.

KARST: Noooo, that's a bit exaggerated.

MALINA: Maybe, but flu vaccines have a 6–13% success rate and they've been around ... I don't know how long.

KARST: Long.
MALINA: Yeah, right.
KARST: Right.
MALINA: And with corona, it has …
KARST: Such a complicated structure and mutating proteins.
MALINA: It's impossible to grab the bull by its horns.
KARST: Exactly!
MALINA: So, I think that's it. It won't go anywhere, it won't be cured or eradicated.
KARST: Just keep getting stronger and more and more devastating …
MALINA: Exactly! So, I think of the children that are incarnating now – how come they want to be born and live maybe ten years only to die …
KARST: Wow, your outlook is so morose. But maybe, if that's the case, it's like "last call, last call, who wants to go play down on Earth. Last chance."
MALINA: Ha ha, so these are the volunteer babies that will walk us into the apocalypse.
KARST: But do you think it really works this way?
MALINA: Of course, every baby chooses.

Scenario 5

KARST: So, what would you like to tell me? That you love me or that you would rather kill me than admit it? Or that, now that you've admitted your love, you gotta kill me?
MALINA: The last one. But just thinking about it makes me severely depressed. I think I'd rather just do myself in.
KARST: Oh come on …
[MALINA *pulls a long nail file out of her purse*]
KARST: Princess! Please, don't be so dramatic! I love you, of course! Tons!
MALINA: Look, I've gone too far, I gotta do it. I gave my word. I take the nail file, I plunge it into my neck vein and I cut it open.
KARST [*this can be acted out as well as narrated*]: No! Malina is shaking. I jump to her, hold her by the shoulders. Hold her while she's trembling. I press her to my heart. She's lost. I start banging with fists and I howl. It is too late.

MALINA'S VOICE [*voice over*]: It's all just a game. But it was a stupid way of exiting the game just when it could be beautiful, and we could be together. Stupid "keep your word." I'm stupid. The saying should mention the exception: don't hold your word if it's *killing yourself* over a young love.

Scenario 6

MALINA: Wait a second Karst, I haven't been completely honest with you.

KARST: Oh, what's up?

MALINA: That I actually care more for you than I'm willing to admit and that I took you seriously.

KARST: What's wrong with that? It's beautiful.

MALINA: Yeah, but I think I've gone too far in my daydreaming, I've lived through all these scenarios and now they're chewed up and I'm over it and I know for sure it wouldn't work anyways.

KARST: Why wouldn't it work?

MALINA: I'm not even sure I have the courage to ask you to be with me, you know, free will and all that.

KARST: Well, I think I would be with you even if I have free will.

MALINA: You're agreeing too much! It has to be because we're in my head (oh my God, perhaps my head is the world, god of this universe). Well anyways, you're agreeing too much.

KARST: Yeah, you like to dominate and maybe I *am* just a figment of your imagination.

MALINA: This reminds me of a nightmare I had as a child. When the prince on a white horse finally entered my dream forest, he was so apathetic or, rather, he so feverishly agreed with what I said or, rather, he wouldn't fight for me, that I woke up all sweaty, kicking the wooden wall. I'm not certain that I didn't get a splinter!

Hey, I actually really think this won't work.

KARST: Why?

MALINA: To be perfectly honest, because I'm disgusting.

KARST: What are you talking about ... We're all a bit gross.

MALINA: Exactly, if I can't put up with my own body, how could I put up with anybody else's?

I probably shouldn't have told you at all.

Scene 2

[*In KARST's car*]

MALINA: Hey, do you remember when we returned from Klagenfurt over the mountain pass?

KARST: From the documentary screening across the border?

MALINA: On the other side, yeah.

KARST: Yeah, I remember, it was a nice ride, a night ride.

MALINA: Yeah, I remember when we arrived back to Ljubljana and stopped at Križanke. The whole night we were followed by a full moon. And when we stopped, I felt like we got stuck in a dream. [*Searching for the right words*] Landed in a dream. No, stuck is better, like we drove to the countryside and got stuck in the mud. [*She nods to herself, like that's a good conclusion*] But we got stuck in the moonlight.

KARST: Did we drive to the countryside to have sex in the fields? Or the woods?

MALINA: It doesn't matter. Listen ...

[*KARST rolls his eyes, starts laughing*]

MALINA: Then, in the moonlight, [*shouts towards the tech booth*] Moonlight filter please! [*The lights change. KARST notices*] I felt as full as the moon. I felt I found you there and really saw you, like you were actually inside of me. It felt like you grew inside of me. And obviously that was such a kiss moment, but I pulled a hundred euros out of my pocket and paid you for running the tech.

KARST: I remember, yup.

MALINA: Maybe it was a bit more than a hundred. I think I added something for the travel expenses.

KARST: Yup.

MALINA: Are you agreeing again?!

KARST: Am I?

MALINA: Just don't overdo it.

KARST: I remember that, I felt "in it" as well.

MALINA: Yeah, it was a feeling like we went to the aquarium to watch the dolphins and in the next moment we were behind the glass and we *were the* dolphins.

[*The light changes to aquarium setting.* MALINA *notices and approvingly nods*]

KARST: Are dolphins aware of themselves?

MALINA: Oh, I've heard everything there is to know about dolphins. They sing, harmonize with each other, have lots of sex, make scientists masturbate them. Apparently, they love pregnant women and they swim to the frontlines if women are giving birth in the ocean and they have magical skills to alleviate the pain of labor and make women come instead.

KARST: What?! Where did you hear that?

MALINA: In the flower of divine ... something ... a known metaphysical text.

KARST: Never heard. Anyways, we're by the colosseum in my car.

[*Both of them look at the lights which turn to the moonlight setting*]

MALINA: Stuck in the mud /

KARST: Or behind the aquarium glass /

MALINA: But I envisioned a gigantic one, with multiple chambers /

KARST: Yeah, as if the entire Madison Square Garden were an aquarium.

[*The lights change to the aquarium setting. They both notice and exclaim*]

MALINA and KARST: *No!* Moonlight.

[*They look at each other. They kiss*]

KARST: Won't Carlos be mad?

MALINA: Won't Claire be mad?

[*They laugh and kiss again*]

MALINA: Look, both their names start with C.

MALINA: But in reality, I paid you and left.

KARST: But then we had a really awesome lunch at the fish restaurant.

MALINA: Yeah, that lunch was crazy! You were looking at me with a special fire in your eyes! Like, your eyes could melt all the Swiss glaciers in that moment.

KARST: Ah, that's why they're melting.

[KARST *tries to make a joke, but* MALINA *doesn't let herself be bothered*]

MALINA: And that's when I asked you if you would go to Siberia with me. 'Cause I had no idea you were a Russiaphile.

KARST: Yup, yup, but I think we went to the fish place before the moonlight.

MALINA: That's perfectly possible, but I think the memory of the Moon claustrofucked all my other memories.

THE END

Ljubimca z medvedom: Okultna komedija o dušah dvojčicah in vlogah, ki jih igramo

MALINA: Ampak, a veš, kdaj sem doumela, da je to nekaj posebnega?

V Makedoniji! Ker sem te bila tako vesela čisto vsakič, ko sem te videla. Ker si tako blazno prezenten in sva v času dvournih zajtrkov dočakala kosilo. To, da te imam rada in bi se vate lahko celo zaljubila, je manj indikativno, da bi midva dejansko lahko bila skupaj, kot pa to, da te lahko prenašam. In to, da sem te noro vesela vsakič, ko te vidim. Pa tudi to je resnica, da sem malo svojeglava, pa nefleksibilna; ti si pa bolj fleksibilen, ampak imaš vseeno integriteto, da me hitro strezniš, ko mimo udarim. Lažje o vsem tem razmišljam, če se pretvarjam, da je moje življenje fikcija.

[*Govorita vse, tudi kar se zdi kot didaskalija v sklopu scenarijev, razen kar je v poševnem tisku. Hkrati vse napotke tudi odigrata. Ob enem je Malina krojačica realnosti, pa tudi igralka*]

MALINA: In zdaj si predstavljam scenarij ena.

Scenarij 1

Obraz se ti popolnoma razsvetli z nasmeškom in me poljubiš, to je to.

[KRAS *jo poljubi*]

Nasmehnem se: V afektirani slovenščini brez regijskih posebnosti.

Bravo. Čudovito si začutil ta moment, ko se v ameriškem filmu poljubita. Ker si filmski režiser, si začutil to, kar je najbolj primerno.

Scenarij 2

MALINA: Obraz se ti popolnoma razsvetli z nasmeškom, seksi provokativno me vprašaš:

KRAS: In v kakšen primeru bi se lahko zaljubila vame?

MALINA [*z nasmeškom zadovoljne princeze*]: Če mi prisežeš, da me ljubiš in da si moj in da bi vse naredil zame.

KRAS: Aha, a ta prisega, to se mora narediti kaj posebnega? Na kolenih?

MALINA: Seveda, na kolenih.

KRAS: Prisegam, da te ljubim in bi zate naredil vse, da bi bila srečna, in izpolnjena ... in ... a je to v redu?

MALINA: Z nasmeškom sramežljivo zadovoljne princeske, ki se iz vznemirjenosti skoraj hihita, dahnem: Ja.

[*Se poljubita. Potem se gledata in smejita*]

MALINA: Ona: se cvileče hihita kot Vila Malina.

KRAS: On: njegovo hecno krohotanje začudenja iz vznemirjenosti, kot da je bil pravkar priča čudežu, kot da bi marjetica rodila pikapolonico. A zdaj si pa zaljubljena?

MALINA: Skomignem z rameni [*mogoče mi je nerodno*].

[*MALINA izbruhne, čeprav se hoče držati nazaj, ni ji ravno prijetno govoriti o tem*]

MALINA: Enkrat sem bila jezna nate, ker me nisi zaščitil. Ko me je on Rus Saša v Sibiriji hotel poseksati, jaz pa njega ne, ko si me kar pustil, ker si narobe prebral signale. Ali pa, ko me je ta drugi Rus hotel poseksati, tudi Saša, v Makedoniji, pa si se tudi umaknil, ker nisi razumel, da jaz hočem tebe! Pa da mene vsi kar naprej hočejo poseksati in da je to za ženske drugače! Ne bomo šle kar z vsakim, ki je navdušen nad nami. Vem pa, da če se ženska meče po moškemu, da se mora to nujno sprejeti. To me je razjezilo manj zaradi konkretnih primerov, in bolj, ker je pričalo o tvojih vrednotah.

Scenarij 3

MALINA: A veš, da če me zavrneš, se ne bova nikoli več videla? Moj ego ne bi prenesel.

KRAS: Pa daj no. Zakaj bi te pa zavrnil?

MALINA: Ja zato, ker se recimo nikoli nočeš z nobeno vezati.

KRAS: Jah, ne ...

MALINA: Mogoče si postal "ta" v moji domišljiji, ker si bil pač edini moški, ki je živel moje idealno življenje z mano; šel na potovanje, delal na mojih umetniških projektih, moški, s katerim lahko govorim o vsem, kar me zanima in lahko grem globoko. No ja, tudi takšen, pred katerim sem videla nagačenega sibirskega volka in pred katerim sem si drznila biti takšna packa, (opa, zdrsnila sem v pravi kliše slovenske dramatike, pogledam v publiko, če je to res predstava in tudi naglas izgovorim vse didaskalije), da sem se sredi sobe polulala v čajnik. Še vedno precej literarno: s tem sem se maščevala slabi pogostitvi moskovskega hotela. Ali se ruskega hotela boljše sliši?

Pravkar sem se zavedla, da je med vsakim prizorom drugačen instagram filter na odru. [*Pogleda* TEHNIKA] A ste to počeli?

TEHNIK: Ja.

MALINA: "By the way" ne vem, če si opazil, da sem rekla "ta", in ne "the one", "tapravi" najbrž v slovenščini, ker sem preveč ošabna in nesigurna. Tega pač ne bi nikoli rekla. Ljubezenske izpovedi so riskantne. In če ne bi bil za, potem bi ti sicer zelo laskalo, ampak če bi ti bila svoboda bolj pomembna, potem bi vseeno rekel ne. Z zajetno dozo prijetnega opravičevanja, ampak čeprav bi ti mogoče oprostila, ti ne bi mogla priznati, da sem ti, ker bi me bilo preveč sram. Da je moški spet zmagal, da sem jaz nekomu priznala svojo ljubezen, on pa je spet rekel: "Ne hvala, ampak ful sem počaščen." Ohhh spet ta bolečina, ko se ti razpara trup in vsi organi ven popadajo in bi najraje, da te pogoltnejo plameni, preden kdo opazi. Itak te je najbolj strah javne osramotitve. Prosim, samo ne objavi na Facebook.

Rehearsing Lines

Cătălina Florina Florescu

Cast

EVE and ANA.

Setting

Here. Two women are seated on a bench. That's all you need to know. Plus, that their names are palindromes – mirrored names. Make what you want out of this.

Time

Now.

EVE: What is the taste of water, dear?
ANA: Excuse me?
EVE: Hard of hearing?
ANA: What?
EVE: Hard of hearing?
ANA: No! Stop that. [*She takes off one of her hearing aids and shows it to the other woman*] I hear fine. I mean. You see ... Aging is no fun.
EVE: How old are you?
ANA: Don't you know that a woman should never reveal her age?
EVE: Well, *if* a man asks, that's when a woman shouldn't reveal her age.
ANA: What's the difference?
EVE: Don't know. That's what I heard.
ANA: I'm 60. Today is my birthday. I am waiting for the bus to take me places.
EVE: You're funny.
ANA: Hysterical.
[*They look at each other. Maybe like observing each other for the first time*]

EVE: Am I real?
ANA: Do you mean like if I can see you? That would be the second stupid question you asked.
EVE: *Thanks*, what was the first one?
ANA: I believe you sat down, looked at me, sighed, and then asked something about the taste of water.
EVE: Oh, I see, you studied me.
ANA: Not really. I've been on this bench for three hours. I have this ritual on my birthday.
EVE: What ritual?
ANA: To meet strangers.
EVE: How many?
ANA: How many what?
EVE: Today, how many did you meet?
ANA: A few. It must be the weather.
EVE: What's wrong with the weather?
ANA: They said there would be a storm later today between the hours of 2:15:32 and 3:45:07. [*Adds as if that could disambiguate*]: PM.
EVE: My, my, precision, precision, precision.
[*They giggle*]
ANA: Look at the sky, though. It's baby blue. Which reminds me …
[ANA *looks for something in her purse. Takes a cell phone out. Starts typing one letter at a time. Very slowly. The other woman is curious but feigns disinterest. Not for long, though.* EVE *stretches her legs and arms. Yawns voraciously. The other gives her a look but goes back to her typing*]
EVE: Are you done?
ANA: With?
EVE: I don't know. That memoir.
ANA: Ah. It's just a reminder to myself to buy something.
EVE: What, a dream house? Judging by the many letters you typed it's something quite exact.
ANA: If you must know, my husband died on my birthday. He loved baby blue and he made me promise that I should try something that color every year. Buy a dress, drink something with blue Curaçao. You know, simple things. Do them, keep a diary, and think of him.

EVE: Nice.

ANA: This is why I sit on this bench. At some point someone has a crazy idea. You just helped me.

EVE: Thanks. [*Perplexed*] Like, how?

ANA: You asked if I knew how the water tasted. Towards the end, my husband was … Well, I'll spare you the details. Imagine a body dying in the same bed where the man made love. He could not taste water. I tried to be supportive. I used to go into the kitchen and drink water from my palms. I couldn't say I knew what the taste of it was. It did not feel special. Why did you ask that?

EVE: Oh, it's nothing.

ANA: Please.

EVE: Well, I have had this cough and nothing that I do helps. I have had so many lozenges, teas, honey, cough syrup, mint drops, chewable vitamin C, soups that, if I have a sip of water, I can't taste it anymore. And I *love* water.

ANA: Sorry, I just don't get what's so special about it.

EVE: Aqua vitae. [*Beat*] I know this cough cannot last forever.

ANA: Have you seen a doctor?

EVE: Yes, a doctor, a pharmacist, and now you.

ANA: Excuse me?

EVE: I don't know why I said that.

ANA: It happens. Words get out of us and we can't delete them.

EVE: I guess.

ANA: Like the other day, I said to this man who was sitting exactly where you sit right now, "Excuse me, do you have the time?" And instead of answering me, guess what he did.

EVE: What?

ANA: He gave me his wristwatch. And I said, "What am I supposed to do with it?" And he said, "I thought you wanted to *have* the time."

EVE: I don't get it.

ANA: Me either. So, I asked him. And he said, "Relax, it's just a joke. I thought you wanted to have the time." Like, really, who can *have* the time? Silly, right?

EVE: Ah, he meant in the literal sense of the word.

ANA [*gestures*]: To have the time. Whatever!

EVE: Look, it's coming.
ANA: What?
EVE: The bus.
ANA: Ah, that's not the one I am waiting for.
EVE: That's the only one that stops here.
ANA: Nope.
EVE: Yes, look over there. It says "Timeline for 123." That's the *only* bus that stops here.
ANA: I'm waiting for bus 321.
EVE: I don't know what are you waiting for. It does not stop here.
ANA: Yes.
EVE: No.
ANA: Yes.
EVE: No! *No!*
[*A moment*]
EVE: Calm down. Where do you want to go?
ANA: I don't know.
EVE: Take a deep breath, it's your birthday, be a good girl.
[*The 123 bus stops. No one gets off. It leaves*]
ANA: Wasn't that your bus?
EVE: It's fine. I'll take the next one.
ANA: There is no next one.
EVE: Of course, there is. It's not midnight. Then they stop.
ANA: But the storm ... the storm is ... is coming.
EVE: No, it's not. It's 4pm. The sky is baby blue. Are you okay?
ANA: The storm is coming. I forgot to feed the cat. I left the window open. The cat may escape. [*No change in her tone*] The cat! The cat! Oh my God, the cat is dead.
EVE: I don't think you are okay. Give me your phone.
ANA: Why?
EVE: To call ... Could someone come to pick you up?
ANA: My cat.
EVE: Be serious.
ANA: My cat. But my cat is dead.
EVE: Fine, don't give me the phone. I have to wait for the bus anyway.
ANA: Where are you going?
EVE: I'm going to see a play.

REHEARSING LINES | *Cătălina Florina Florescu*

ANA: Lovely. Which play?
EVE: "Six Characters in Search of an Author."
ANA: Will it ever end?
EVE: Excuse me???
ANA: This search.
EVE: Huh?
ANA: For illusions. [*One more time and slower*] This ... search ... for ... illusions.
EVE: Don't spoil it for me.
ANA: The illusion? ... The reality?
EVE [*changing the subject*]: Say, do you really have a cat?
ANA: Had.
EVE: *Did* you have a cat?
ANA: Maybe. [*A bit childish*] I don't want to tell you. I don't know you.
EVE: True. You did tell me it was your birthday and that your husband ...
ANA: Did you meet my husband?
EVE: Oh my God! You are batshit [*gestures crazy*].
ANA: I am perfectly fine. Everybody knew my husband.
EVE: Is that so?
ANA: Of course.
EVE: What was his name?
ANA: Pete.
EVE: Pete Jr., the great, the mighty..., Pete what?
ANA: Just Pete.
EVE: Never mind.
ANA: He was a star.
EVE: I'm sure.
ANA: He serenaded all beautiful women of the city.
EVE: Lucky me, I am not.
ANA: Yes, of course you are. *All* women are beautiful!
EVE [*trying to play her game*]: Well, let's just say I met Pete.
ANA [*excited*]: Yes!
EVE: What do you want to know?
ANA: How was he?
EVE: How was ... ?
ANA: In bed, silly.

EVE: Oh, he was the best. Sorry for my indiscretion.
ANA: Did he bring you flowers?
EVE: Always.
ANA: Which kind?
EVE: Roses.
ANA: That son of a bitch! He never brought me flowers. He said they would die too soon.
EVE: Why did *he* die?
ANA: How should I know?
EVE: Didn't you say ... ?
ANA: I don't know what you heard. [*Turns her head in the opposite direction. After a few seconds*] Do I know you from somewhere?
EVE: No. I am not famous.
ANA: My name is Ana. So nice to talk to someone.
EVE: I'm sorry, but my bus is coming.
ANA: I see no bus.
EVE: Well, that's fine. I'll walk.
ANA: Too bad. We could have kept each other company.
EVE: Another time.
ANA: What are the chances to meet again?
EVE: Slim. Like today's storm.
ANA: Exactly. Stay. *Please.*
EVE: I gotta go. I am late.
ANA: Late for what?
EVE: Theater.
ANA: Ah, forget about theater. Those characters will still be searching tomorrow for a ... reality. Or illusion. It never ends.
EVE: I have nonrefundable tickets.
ANA: Tickets? Are you going with someone?
EVE: Yes. I'm late.
ANA: How lucky. To have someone. Go, hurry up.
EVE: Bye. Eat cake.
ANA: Why?
EVE: It's your birthday, isn't it?
[*EVE leaves. It becomes foggy. Like in a dream. Like on stage. Like in who wants to get old and lonely?!*]
ANA: The taste of water. [*Takes her phone. Dictates to it*] What is the taste of water? [*Puts the phone back in her purse*] That's a good

icebreaker. I should use it next time. How do I look? [*Takes a mirror out of her pocket. A lipstick. Sings something. Stops because she forgot parts of the lyrics. Resumes from where she interrupted herself. She still can't remember the lyrics but, instead of stopping, she ad-libs*]

THE END

Κάνοντας πρόβα

χαρακτήρεσ

ΕΥΑ και ΑΒΑ.

Δύο γυναίκες σε ένα παγκάκι. Αυτό είναι το μόνο που χρειάζεται να γνωρίζεις. Επίσης τα ονόματά τους είναι παλίνδρομο. Ονόματα που καθρεφτίζονται. Ό,τι καταλαβαίνεις

ΕΥΑ: Ποια είναι η γεύση του νερού, αγαπητή.
ΑΒΑ: Τι εννοείς.
ΕΥΑ: Έχεις ακούσει την ακοή.
ΑΒΑ: Τι.
ΕΥΑ: Άκουσες την ακοή.
ΑΒΑ: Όχι! Σταμάτα. [*Βγάζει το ένα βοήθημα ακοής και το δείχνει στην άλλη γυναίκα*] Ακούω μια χαρά. Εννοώ. Βλέπεις... Τα γηρατειά δεν έχουν πλάκα.
ΕΥΑ: Πόσο χρονών είσαι.
ΑΒΑ: Δεν ξέρεις πως μια γυναίκα δεν πρέπει ποτέ να ΕΥΑγγελίζεται ΕΥΑειδώς την ηλικία της.
ΕΥΑ: Λοιπόν, *αν κάποιος άντρας ρωτήσει*, τότε μια γυναίκα δεν είναι ΕΥΑειδώς καλό να τη λέει.
ΑΒΑ: Ποια είναι η διαφορά.
ΕΥΑ: Δεν ξέρω. Αυτό άκουσα.
ΑΒΑ: Είμαι εξήντα. Σήμερα είναι τα γενέθλιά μου. Περιμένω το περιοδικό για να πάει βόλτα.
ΕΥΑ: Έχεις πλάκα.
ΑΒΑ: Τρομερή.

[Κοιτάνε η μία την άλλη. Σαν να παρατηρούν η μία την άλλη για πρώτη φορά]

ΕΥΑ: Είμαι πραγματική.

ΑΒΑ: Εννοείς αν μπορώ να σε δω; Αυτή είναι η δεύτερη πιο χαζή ερώτησή σου.

ΕΥΑ: Ευχαριστώ, ποια ήταν η πρώτη.

ΑΒΑ: ΕΒΑγγελίζομαι πως ήταν όταν έκατσες κάτω, με κοίταξες, αναστέναξες, και μετά με ρώτησες κάτι για τη γεύση του νερού.

ΕΥΑ: Α, μάλιστα, με μελέτησες.

ΑΒΑ: Όχι ιδιαίτερα. Είμαι σε αυτό το παγκάκι για τρεις ώρες. Έχω αυτό το τελετουργικό στα γενέθλιά μου.

ΕΥΑ: Τι τελετουργικό.

ΑΒΑ: Να συναντάω αγνώστους.

ΕΥΑ: Πόσους.

ΑΒΑ: Πόσους τι?

ΕΥΑ: Σήμερα, πόσους συνάντησες.

ΑΒΑ: Λίγους. Πρέπει να ήταν ο καιρός.

ΕΥΑ: Τι πρόβλημα υπάρχει με τον καιρό.

ΑΒΑ: Είπαν πως θα έχει μια καταιγίδα σήμερα, αργότερα, ανάμεσα στις 2:15:32 και 3:45:07. [*Και προσθέτει σαν με αμφιβολία*] ΜΜ.

ΕΥΑ: Πω, πω, ακρίβεια, ακρίβεια.

[Χαχανίζουν]

ΑΒΑ: Κοίτα τον ουρανό. Είναι ένα παιδικό γαλάζιο. Που μου θυμίζει ...

(Translated by Zafiris Nikitas)

Cerebrum

Avery Grace

Cast

P.F.SÍ or the prefrontal cortex (rules cognitive control functions such as attention, impulse inhibition, thinking into the future, cognitive flexibility): an aloof character who tends to rationalize out loud and attempt to talk his way into calmness. Is privileged and upset when no one listens to him. Tends towards immediate conflict with both LIMBY and A. MYGDÁLA

A. MYGDÁLA or the amygdala (senses threats and activates fear-related responses such as fight, flight, freeze, and shut down): older, masculine, testy; tends toward hyperarousal. Married to LIMBY

LIMBY or the limbic system (mediates between cerebral cortex and the amygdala; responsible for arousal and memory, as well as voluntary choices such as fighting and fleeing): skittish/worrisome/hysterical, femme (*à la* Nathan Lane in *The Birdcage*) always comparing whatever event happens to some experience she had before a given situation

HIPPO or the hippocampus (stores long-term memories and ideally makes them resistant to forgetting; this goes offline until stress): forgetful, cannot concentrate, has abrupt flashbacks where they lose speech. Sibling of HYPO

HYPO or the hypothalamus (controls hormonal system, sends signals to pituitary to release them): overtalkative, cannot stop talking, always "secreting something" on hearing bad news. "That makes me _____." The peacemaker once everyone "up top" (prefrontal cortex, limbic system, amygdala) cannot calm down or stop conflicting. Sibling of HIPPO

PIT or the pituitary gland (the "master gland" that releases hormones at behest of the hypothalamus): best friend with HYPO, they are "joined at the hip." Follower to a fault and overproduces and over-agrees with HYPO.

Avery Grace | CEREBRUM

Setting

A single room with one door.

[*Lights come up on a single room with one door. All the cast is passing time, waiting around for something unknown.* LIMBY *and* A. MYGDÁLA, *a couple, are sitting at a small table playing cards together.* P.F.SÍ *stands against the wall and always stands above the other characters or paces around the room throughout the act.* HIPPO *and* HYPO—*siblings and the latter who eats and talks compulsively between bites—are sitting at another table with* PIT *sitting next to* HYPO *on same side of the table. There is an old corded rotary telephone on one wall*]

LIMBY [*plays a card, then pauses. Looks to each character while speaking nervously*]: Suh, suh, so ... [*pauses again*] has anyone heard anything yet?

P.F.SÍ [*leans against wall near* LIMBY *and* A. MYGDÁLA's *table, looks at watch*]: Nothing yet. But there must be some kind of rational explanation.

A. MYGDÁLA [*plays his card in turn. Speaks antagonistically to P.F.*]: C'mon, you *always* say that. Whaddayou know? [*Gestures to* LIMBY] For all *you* know, my Limby here could be right to be nervous. Better ready than surprised. [*Plays another card*] It's not like we know what's comin'.

P.F.SÍ. [*puts his hands up defensively*]: Hey hey, no need to get uppity now. I'm just saying the same as you – we don't know anything yet. For all we know things could be fine.

A. MYGDÁLA: They could also *not* be fine too. Have ya thought about that? [*Slams hands on table while leaning forward towards P.F.*] You think you're smarter than the rest of us?! ... Huh, dontcha?!

P.F.SÍ. [*shakes head in frustration*]: I hate it when you get like this. You're impossible to talk to. A caustic wall. [*Walks to other side of room away from the card table, then looks at watch again*]

LIMBY: Oh! You're both making so me nervous! Why are you two always fighting?! I'm always caught in the middle!

CEREBRUM | *Avery Grace*

A. MYGDÁLA [*to* LIMBY]: I'm sorry, baby. I'll try to tone it down. Besides, we can always get outta here if need be. I'm not afraid to run if we need to. [*Gestures to door, rubs her leg*]

HIPPO [*puts index finger in the air*]: Oh! Hey, y'all, I sort of remember ... wait, shit, I forgot ... Gimme a minute. [*Holds his temples with his hand, lightly taps his own head afterwards*] God, I get so forgetful. I hate it ...

A. MYGDÁLA: God damn it, c'mon, out with it, Hippo! [*Looks at* LIMBY, *catches self, settles down*] Shit, I'm sorry, baby. *Again.*

HYPO [*between bites, drools/froths when he speaks*]: Hey, hey! No need to shout. We're right here and you're getting *all of us* amped up! You've got me eating and spilling so much I can hardly stand it!

PIT: Yeah! Me too!

HYPO: Shut up, Pit.

A. MYGDÁLA: Yeah, shut up, Pit. You always agree with what he says.

PIT: So what? He's usually right. And even if he wasn't, haven't you heard of loyalty? [*Swoons*]

HIPPO: If y'all would just shut up for a minute I might be able to remember! [*Pauses*] Ahh, right! I remember now. [*Checks phone*] I got this text ... it says, "Don't move. BRT" ... [*scratches head*] What's BRT again? [*Looks around at others*]

LIMBY: It means, "be right there"! What do you think that means??

P.F.SÍ.: Uh ... be, right there? Duh. [*Rolls eyes visibly*] Isn't it *obvious*?

LIMBY: But, but, what does *right there* mean?? And who?? Or what? Who or what will *be right there*?? Right here?!

A. MYGDÁLA: Don't worry, baby. If anything crazy happens, I'll take care of ya. [*Puts up his fists in gesture, his cell phone rings, he picks up*] Hello? Yes, this is A. Mygdála. Who's this? [*Pauses*] Oh ... I see. Well ... yeah. Sure. I'll tell the others. [*Hangs up phone, becomes visibly shaken*] They uh ... uh ...

LIMBY: What, sweetie?! Who was it?! What is it?!

A. MYGDÁLA: They ... they said not to go anywhere. They said to stay put ... *or else.*

LIMBY: Or else?! Or else, what?! Ahh! It's happening again, I just know it! [*Looks to* A. MYGDÁLA *to comfort her but this time he* doesn't but starts to look glazed over/goes into freeze/shut down mode] Honey? Honey?! [A. MYGDÁLA *falls out of his seat onto the floor in a freeze state*, LIMBY *comes down to check on him*] Honey!! [*Looks up and around at other characters*] He's frozen! Somebody do something!

P.F.SÍ.: Oh, shit! [*Runs over to their table, kneels down, checks his neck pulse and then puts ear to his mouth*] He's still with us, he's breathing. [*Looks to Limby*] Who called?

LIMBY [*looks at* A. MYGDÁLA's *phone*]: It says "unknown caller". [*Holds hand to mouth*] It's a blocked number!

P.F.SÍ.: What about location? It usually says where the call or the phone account is from.

HYPO [*speaks with a full mouth*]: Oh man, all this is making me crazy nervous. [*Looks around*] Is there a bathroom here somewhere? I swear, I'm about to explode.

PIT: Yeah, me too!

HYPO: Shut up, Pit. I'm f-in' serious.

LIMBY: You're serious?! *This* is serious!

P.F.SÍ.: Limby! [*Shakes her by the shoulders/arms*] Stay calm. We need you rational for this. Now, did the phone say where the call was from?

LIMBY: Oh! [LIMBY *checks phone again*] No, it doesn't say anything! Isn't it supposed to say *something*?! I don't understand! I just know that this is bad! [A. MYGDÁLA *groans*, LIMBY *looks back to him*] Oh! Sweetie!

P.F.SÍ. [*stands up*]: Like I said, there's gotta be some kind of explanation. So, what do we know? [*Counts on his fingers*] One – someone or something is coming. Two – they, it, whatever, doesn't want us to go anywhere ... or else. [*Pauses*] So it could be anything ... [*Speaks as if trying to persuade himself*] Something good or fine is just as possible as something bad ... right? I mean, let's not lose our heads here.

HYPO: What do you mean *don't lose our heads*? That's exactly what you're all doing! They said, "or else." How could we not go apeshit??

PIT: Yeah! Apeshit!

HYPO: Shut up, Pit!

P.F.SÍ.: Yeah, shut up, Pit!

CEREBRUM | *Avery Grace*

HYPO [*long and loud sigh*]: God damn it ... now part of me feels like I have to clean this up somehow. But honestly, part of me would rather jump on the fear train with you all. [*Pauses*] I swear, it's like having an angel and a devil on each shoulder. [*Sighs*] *Exhausting ...*

PIT: So exhausting!

HYPO [*angry sigh*]: For fuck's sake ... shut up, Pit!

HIPPO and P.F.SÍ [*look at one another and say in unison*]: Not even gonna touch that one ...

P.F.SÍ. [*said with suspicion*]: Wait. Hippo. You said you got a text from them before. Did you talk to them?

HIPPO [*holds both temples*]: I wish ... I wish I could remember ...

P.F.SÍ. [*pace-circles around HIPPO*]: Maybe A. Mygdála was right ... c'mon, out with it!

HIPPO: Look, I'm sorry! I get really forgetful when I'm scared, okay?! Like, totally blank. [*Stares off into space*]

HYPO [*sighs*]: Like I said, now it's my job to save the day. *Again.* Besides, Hippo's not going to remember any better if you yell at her!

PIT: Yeah! Not gonna remember better!

WHOLE CAST minus PIT and A. MYGDÁLA: *Shut up, Pit!*

PIT: ... alright, geez. [*Looks down*] I guess I just won't say anything from now on ... [*Pouts*]

HYPO: *Great.* I mean, at times it's great to have you next to me, Pit, but ... sometimes ... well, you know, I kinda wish I didn't have to do all the thinking and talking. [*PIT looks down and stays silent. HYPO looks expectantly at PIT while speaking*] Piiiiiiiit? Cmon, Pit. It's true. But I can't do it without you. Can't do much of anything. [*Pause*] I'm the inspiration, you're the manifestation. Right? C'mon ... will you please forgive me?

PIT [*looks up*]: Forgive you?

HYPO: Yeah.

PIT: Yeah, I'll forgive you. [*Smiles*]

P.F.SÍ.: Oh my god, Pit, shut up. You're such a follower, it's nauseating ...

HYPO: Shut up, P.F.SÍ!

PIT: Yeah! Shut up, P.F.SÍ!

P.F.SÍ.: Christ. Now there's two of them.

LIMBY: May I remind you that there's someone or something coming! And they've said, "or else"! [A. MYGDÁLA *groans again and starts to come to*] Honey! You're back!

A. MYGDÁLA [*blinks, shakes his head, sits up dazed, then becomes a little aggravated*]: God, I hate it when that happens! How long was I out this time?

LIMBY: Just a couple minutes. But too long for me!

A. MYGDÁLA: I'm sorry, baby, I didn't mean to worry you. It won't happen again. I'll fight it if I have to. [P.F.SÍ.'s *phone buzzes,* A. MYGDÁLA *looks in his direction*] What is it? Who is it? What'd they say?

P.F.SÍ. [*answers his phone*]: Hello? Yeah. What? Three minutes? You'll be here in three minutes? Who are you?! Why are you doing this?! Tell us why you're doing this! Hello? Hello?! [*Looks at phone in frustration, hangs up*]

LIMBY: Gah! It's happening again. Just like *last time!* I can't do this again! [*looks at* P.F.SÍ] Why do they have your number?? You're with them, aren't you?! Honey, get him!

A. MYGDÁLA [*glares at* P.F.SÍ]: Is my Limby right? Are you with them? You are, aren't you!

P.F.SÍ.: Whoa, whoa, whoa! You're both being paranoid! Just 'cause they called me doesn't mean I'm with them. [*Points at* A. MYGDÁLA *and then* HIPPO] Remember, you and Hippo got texts or calls from them too! And Limby even said it's happening like last time! What was last time?

HIPPO: Wha ... what?? [*Looks off into space*] I ... can't ... remember ...

A. MYGDÁLA: That's just what they would say! I mean, well ... [*Look of resignation*] I suppose you're right ...

P.F.SÍ.: Um, wait, what? Are you ... agreeing with me?

A. MYGDÁLA: I never thought I'd say this but ... yes. You're right. [*Straightens his clothes*] So what? I mean, so now what? They'll be here any moment. What do we do?

P.F.SÍ.: I, uh, I don't know what to do with that. I guess we ... um, well ... we have to stand together. All of us.

LIMBY: Like, literally stand together? Or metaphorically?

P.F.SÍ.: I mean, a reasonable person would've gone with metaphor but I suppose we could stand together literally.

CEREBRUM | *Avery Grace*

HYPO: Oh my god, I thought you'd never ask. We absolutely need to stand together. [*Finishes chewing*] So I don't have to stand for you all.

PIT: Yeah, stand together!

HYPO and P.F.SÍ. [*each puts a hand on either of PIT's shoulders*]: I guess you don't have to shut up this time, Pit.

PIT: Ah, really? You see, I was getting really disheartened there for a second, being criticized all the time. I'm glad you all came to your senses. I mean, I'm pretty essential [*looks to HYPO*] Hypo, you don't have to solve everything this time. Let me produce something here that might help us. [*HYPO and P.F.SÍ look at each other with bewilderment, then back to PIT*]

P.F.SÍ.: So, uh, Pit ... [*shakes head*] what did you have in mind?

PIT: So as you said, we gotta stand together. Which leaves two questions: how do we settle our differences? And what does standing together look like? Like is it literally standing together when "they" [*does air quotes*] arrive? What do we do there? I think it's incumbent on us to come together.

P.F.SÍ.: *Huh.* This is a great idea. Practical. I guess it makes sense for me to start [*looks at LIMBY and A. MYGDÁLA*] Limby, Mygdála, I know I can be a little aloof, arrogant, and dismissive at times, especially to you two. I'm sorry, and I commit to doing it better.

A. MYGDÁLA: You're right and it's about time. [*LIMBY elbows him in the side, he grunts but doesn't say anything*]

LIMBY: Honey, he's *apologizing* ... shut your trap. [*Looks to P.F.SÍ*] Thank you for your apology and your reassurance. I know I can be a worry wart, and a tad hysterical. [*Looks intently at A. MYGDÁLA*] I'll try to rein it in.

A. MYGDÁLA [*audible, annoyed sigh*]: ... yeah ... me too. I know I'm a little testy.

P.F.SÍ. [*jokingly*]: Just a little?

HYPO: Hey, folks! What about us over here?

PIT: Yeah! Us over here.

P.F.SÍ, LIMBY, and A. MYGDÁLA: Sorry we make you clean up our messes. [*All look at PIT*] And sorry, Pit, for telling you to shut up.

HYPO and PIT: Thank you. We'll try to keep the ... overproduction down, so to speak. Stick to a little ... *regulation*.

Avery Grace | CEREBRUM

P.F.SÍ.: Alright, well, that just leaves one of us left. [*Looks at* HIPPO, *then to the rest of the cast, addressing them*] Do we even apologize to Hippo? I mean, will she even remember right now, you know what I mean? [*Whole cast laughs*]
HYPO: I mean what do we have to lose?
WHOLE CAST minus HIPPO: Sorry, Hippo!
HIPPO: Huh? Sorry for what? Wait ... where am I?
LIMBY [*looks at* P.F.SÍ]: Like you said.
A. MYGDÁLA: That's my baby.
P.F.SÍ.: Well, about any minute now. It seems like if each of us just does what we're best at then, then that's the way we stand together.
LIMBY: Sounds reasonable. Besides, what else are we going to do [*looking at* A. MYGDÁLA *then the rest of the cast, cast wordlessly gets up, stands facing the door. They pause, each looking back and forth to the others in turn*]
[*There is the sound of loud footsteps "outside the door." A loud clink, then turning of a key, ending with a slam. Door starts to open slowly*]
P.F.SÍ.: Here we go, I guess!
LIMBY: I'm glad we did that otherwise I'd be so nervous!
HYPO: You're welcome! I'm glad to finally not have to take care of the mess all myself!
PIT: Yeah, myself!
WHOLE CAST: Shut up, Pit!
A. MYGDÁLA: Ah, shit.
[*Door continues to open, house lights go down on the cast holding hands facing the door, ending the scene*]

THE END

Cerebro

LIMBY [*juega una carta y luego hace una pausa. Mira a los demás personajes mientras habla nerviosamente*]: Pues ... [*hace pausa una vez más*] ¿Alguien ha escuchado algo ya?

CEREBRUM | *Avery Grace*

P.F.SÍ [*se inclina contra la pared cerca de la mesa de* LIMBY *and* A. MYGDÁLA *y mira a su reloj*]: Nada todavía. Pero obviamente debe haber alguna explicación racional.

A. MYGDÁLA [*juega una carta en su turno. Habla de forma antagónica con* P.F.SÍ]: ¡Vamos, siempre dices eso! ¿Qué sabes tú? [*Le hace un gesto a* LIMBY] Por lo que sabes, mi Limby tiene razón al estar nerviosa. Es mejor estar preparados que sorprendernos. [*Juega una carta más*] No es que no sepamos lo que viene.

P.F.SÍ [*levanta sus manos de forma defensiva*]: ¡Oye! No hay necesidad de alterarse ahora. Yo simplemente estoy diciendo lo mismo que tú: aún no sabemos nada. Por lo que sabemos, las cosas podrían salir bien.

A. MYGDÁLA: Pero también podrían no estar bien. ¿Has pensado en eso? [*Golpea las manos contra la mesa Mientras se inclina hacia* P.F.SÍ] ¡Crees que eres más listo que el resto de nosotros!, ¿verdad?

P.F.SÍ [*sacude la cabeza con frustración*]: Odio cuando te pones así. Es imposible hablar contigo. Una pared cáustica. [*Camina hacia el otro lado de la habitación, lejos de la mesa de cartas, luego mira el reloj de nuevo*]

LIMBY: ¡Oh! ¡Ustedes dos me están poniendo tan nerviosa! ¡¿Por qué siempre están peleando?! ¡Siempre estoy atrapada en el medio!

A. MYGDÁLA [*a* LIMBY]: Lo siento, amor. Voy a tratar de bajar el tono. Además, siempre podemos irnos de aquí si lo necesitamos. No tengo miedo de correr si es necesario.

HIPPO [*levanta su dedo índice en el aire*]: ¡Oh! Escúchenme todos, creo que recuerdo un poco ... Mierda ... Espérenme, lo olvidé ... Denme un minuto. [*Se sujeta las sienes con sus manos y luego golpea ligeramente su cabeza*] Dios, soy tan olvidadizo. Lo odio ...

A. MYGDÁLA: ¡Maldita sea, vamos, suéltalo, Hippo! [*Mira a* LIMBY, *la calma y la tranquiliza*] Mierda, lo siento, amor. Otra vez.

HYPO [*entre bocado y bocado, babea mientras habla*]: ¡Oye, oye! No hace falta gritar. ¡Estamos justo aquí y nos estás asustando a todos! ¡Me haces comer y derramar tanto que no lo soporto!

PIT: ¡Sí, a mí también!

HYPO: Cállate, Pit.

A. MYGDÁLA: Sí, cállate, Pit. Siempre estás de acuerdo con lo que dice él.

PIT: ¿Y qué? Por lo general, suele tener razón. Y aunque no la tuviera, ¿no sabes lo que es la lealtad? [*Se desmaya*]

HIPPO: ¡Si todos se callaran por un momento podría ser capaz de recordar! [*Hace una pausa*] ¡Ah! Ya lo recuerdo. [*Revisa su teléfono*] Tengo este texto ... Dice: "No te muevas. BRT" [*Se rasca la cabeza*] ¿Qué es BRT? [*Mira alrededor a los demás*]

LIMBY: ¡Quiere decir "estaré allí" en inglés! ¿Qué creen que significa eso?

P.F.SÍ: Mmm ... ¿Estaré allí? Obviamente. [*Revolea los ojos notablemente*] ¿No es obvio?

LIMBY: Pero, pero, ¿qué significa "allí"? ¿Y quién? ¿O qué? ¿Qué o quién va a estar "allí"? ¿Aquí mismo?!

A. MYGDÁLA: No te preocupes, amor. Si sucede alguna locura, yo te cuidaré. [*Levanta los puños haciendo un gesto, su teléfono móvil suena y él lo coge*] ¿Hola? Sí, soy A. Mygdála. ¿Quién es? [*Hace una pausa*] Oh ... Ya veo. Bueno ... Sí, por supuesto. Se lo diré a los demás. [*Cuelga el teléfono y se agita notablemente*] Ellos, eh ... Eh ...

LIMBY: ¡¿Qué, cariño?! ¡¿Quién era?! ¡¿Qué sucede?!

A. MYGDÁLA: Ellos ... Ellos dicen que no vayamos a ninguna parte. Dicen que nos quedemos aquí o de lo contrario...

A Turkey Is Not a Rooster

Jinna Kim

Cast

ROOSTER: protagonist, 20–30-year-old full-time office dud (any gender) and part-time interdisciplinary artist

DRAGON: nemesis, older white female, 50–60 years old, founder and director of Sunny Days Zoo

DOG/PUPPY: minion, Dragon's young assistant 15–25 years old, any gender

NARRATOR (OPTIONAL): any age, any gender.

Setting

USA. The present.

NARRATOR: Last Christmas, after seeing a Facebook post requesting a Rooster artist, our protagonist Rooster excitedly schedules a Zoom call while munching on leftover winter solstice festival Dongzhi dumplings and rice cakes.

ROOSTER: Cock-a-doodle-do! Hi Dragon lady, super excited to audition as a Rooster performer. I majored in Circus Arts in undergrad. I work on a remote farm, so if the internet gets wonky, I will reconnect right away. Confirming you got my headshot and full body photo for species verification?

DRAGON: Yes, thank you for the resume and photos. My minion, my puppy dog, tells me that your experience is "authentic." I can screen share our recorded Zoom newsletter which will tell you a bit about the project and you can tell me if you are interested in becoming part of my circus.

DOG [*in Zoom recording*]: Zoom news – woof! Woof! We at Sunny Days Traveling Zoo, have successfully assembled a diverse troupe of animals to develop an exciting performance montage. Funded by various sponsors, this circus-inspired show will be performed at venues throughout North America in 2020. Issues of diversity and inclusion of species aren't highlighted enough, not anywhere near often enough. This ensemble strives to show an honest and insightful look at the animals we love from our past and present.

ROOSTER: Yes! Great news, I am *so* interested in becoming part of your circus!

DRAGON: Welcome Rooster to my circus troupe of delicious, I mean diverse animals. As you will see, we are still in a rough draft process. Please feel free to see what has been recorded so far and start contributing online!

NARRATOR: They quickly agree over Zoom and after the call ends, Rooster leaves his video on and does a happy winter solstice dance, using the computer screen as a mirror. Note at this point no time commitments or official paperwork was discussed or signed. Soon after Rooster completes his circus piece in record time and repeats his happy winter solstice in front of the mirror.

DRAGON [*starts new Zoom call with circus performers*]: Hi animals, I need to eat, I mean I need to meet with the entire circus troupe again in two months – to prepare for our meeting with major human donors. For those still making edits, I will have individual conversations to naturally, assert my dominance.

ROOSTER [*mutes Zoom*]: Still making edits?! My work is complete perfection *and* more *original*. What the flock?! What is this fluff that the other animals came up with, and what is taking them *so long*? Regardless my unique cocks will be heard, and my birdbrain will soon be known far beyond Charlotte, NC ... me, me, me!!!

NARRATOR: Dragon tries to muffle her growling stomach and snorts quietly "enough already, feasting time will come soon enough" along with a few flames.

DRAGON: So, in closing, *friendly* reminder that our dress rehearsal for the human donors is *mandatory*. Please look at the shared document and be sure that your final choreography and vocals, if applicable, are included before then. I will assign the master chef/ringleader, order, timing and such for the dress rehearsal. Thank you for your species' meaty contributions to my project. Puppy will be sure to fetch the human refreshments. And bananas. B-A-N-A-N-A-S!

A TURKEY IS NOT A ROOSTER | Jinna Kim

NARRATOR: The winter festival rehearsal for rich donors goes better than expected which consequently increases overall feed [*with fancier rice cakes and dumplings*] for the circus and *more* tour dates. Observant Rooster urges copyrighting the circus show – since it is an original compilation.

DRAGON [*asked ROOSTER to join the next Zoom call early*]: I am so glad an avian with our kind of birdbrain has joined our group!

DRAGON [*still on Zoom now addressing entire animal troupe*]: We have tripled the number of donors, sponsors, and performances. Our work has been successfully copyrighted thanks to Rooster. Also, I will negotiate all pay and housing on tour and fatten your feed. Oh, and I have some other animals interested in auditioning for your roles.

DOG: Woof! Woof! Woof! Good evening circus troupe! Hope you're all doing well. The following rehearsal dates are as follows: every weekend for the next year. The frequency of rehearsals and meals will obviously increase prior to each performance.

ROOSTER [*just before the Zoom call ends for the troupe*]: Hey Dragon and Puppy can we please stay on the Zoom call for a couple minutes with just the three of us? I only have three lines and my original chicken dance. I work more than 40 hours a week at a mega farm, so given the ten-hour commute to our rehearsal space, I can only commit to one rehearsal per month, before each performance. Since you got an understudy, can't they be my stand-in? I also emailed you a recording of all of my lines and triumphant dance. Isn't that enough?

DRAGON: *No, not* enough flesh present! I was afraid that may be the case and knew that some of the animals would not be able to continue to perform their own work. I would like to recast you and, of course, give you credit for the avian writing and meaty choreography that is copyrighted. The nature of the performance makes copious rehearsal time as a troupe necessary. I appreciate your birdbrain contributions. Please email me your address so that I can mail you a check for five cents. And Puppy will fetch you some gummy worms for your previous long commutes.

ROOSTER [*at the beginning of a new Zoom group call*]: Cock-a-doodle-doo fellow animals and humans! Not sure if anyone else

Jinna Kim | A TURKEY IS NOT A ROOSTER

was replaced, but just wanted to let y'all know that I did not quit but was removed behind my tailfeathers since I can't make all the rehearsals. I also asked if my understudy could be my stand-in. Ironically it was my idea to copyright our circus show, and now I hope you won't repeat the Avian Exclusion Act of 1882. I feel like this opportunity was a bait and switch, in that I was invited to develop the avian perspective as an avian writer and performer, but that has been gobbled away.

DRAGON: Oh Rooster, Rooster – the animal, your understudy, who replaced you is a young Turkey. We always cast the roles authentically. [*Mutes Zoom so others cannot hear*] Rooster has big brains, small body. Turkey has small brains, big body ha ha.

NARRATOR: Dragon continues to mumble "gobble gobble," licks her lips, and snorts tiny flames.

ROOSTER [*still on the same Zoom call*]: What the flock?! I feel baited, switched, and exploited. None of you actually spoke to me and everyone seems to have used my birdbrain. Without my knowledge, I was replaced by another avian, by a fat Turkey and removed from the Facebook circus group? I returned my five-cent artist paycheck. Culturally, I am still shocked.

DOG [*mutters after muting Zoom*]: A Turkey is not a Rooster? Cock-a-doodle-doo and gobble gobble are close enough.

DRAGON: Why *yes*, we have decided to replace you as both an avian writer and performer. *All* of us wish you the best.

DOG [*DOG and DRAGON stay on call with DOG chewing on bone*]: So ... we can never tell Rooster that we replaced him with a Turkey because we roast the bird alive every performance while it dances? *Yum*, turkeys are a better replacement anyway, more meat for the penny. Dime a dozen. Gobble Gobble!

DRAGON: *Yes*, and only the Rooster had the brains to ask about paperwork. We can never be sued directly since all the carnivores and omnivores keep gobbling the evidence like there's no tomorrow!

NARRATOR: Dragon can be seen dashing through the snow, flapping her wings.

DOG [*in a video recording*]: *Woof! Woof! Zoom news Zoom news!* Everybody, what you see on our website is true – all Sunny Days shows have been postponed or canceled due to the coronavirus.

However, there are disinfectant wipes, antibacterial soaps, and chewing bones, still available onsite at our headquarters.

NARRATOR: Epilogue – the copyright included Rooster as an original writer and cast member. Even after the new year, Rooster continues to perform his original piece "A Turkey is *not* a Rooster," as a solo act. While it continues to sell out online, a new character – the Peacock, starts copycatting Rooster's mannerisms including his happy winter solstice dance, for Peacock's new theater piece titled "Dongzhi Birds" which has already lined up gigs at more prestigious institutions, for higher pay and haute cuisine.

THE END

터키는 수탉이 아니다

발문 - 저작권에는 원작자이자 출연진인 수탉가 포함되어 있습니다. 수탉는 새해에도 솔로곡 "터키는 수탉이 아니다"를 솔로 활동으로 이어간다. 온라인에서는 품절이 계속되고 있는 가운데, 새로운 캐릭터 공작이 더 높은 급여를 위해 이미 더 유명 기관에서 공연을 하고 있는 공작의 새 연극 작품 "동지 조류"를 위해 행복한 동지 춤을 포함한 수탉의 매너를 모방하기 시작합니다. 그리고 고급 요리.

Bottle Man: A Comedy

Elena Naskova

Cast

MURIEL: a woman in her forties
MAN: a man in his thirties.

Setting

Muriel's living room. There is a sofa, a coffee table, and a trashcan in the room. Clothes, magazines, and papers are scattered all over the place.

Scene 1

[MURIEL *enters. She throws her bag on the sofa and sits down. She takes off her shoes and massages her feet*]

MURIEL: These shoes are going to put me in a wheelchair. [MURIEL *takes off her socks. She smells them. She makes a face and throws them on the floor*]

MURIEL: Toxic waste!

[MURIEL *reaches inside her bag and pulls out an old, corked bottle. She carefully examines the bottle and attempt to clean it with her sleeve*]

MURIEL: A piece of garbage-souvenir from Golden Hills. And I picked it up, why?

[MURIEL *throws the bottle in the trashcan. She searches through a pile of magazines pulls one. She looks through it*]

MURIEL: I love this double-fleece wrap robe ... over these silk pajamas ... But ... I've maxed-out my credit cards. I can't buy it.

[MURIEL *throws the magazine on floor*]

MURIEL: I don't need it, anyway. I live alone. Who cares what I'm wearing at home, or not wearing. I could walk around naked if I wanted to, as long as it's dark in here, so I can't get a glimpse of my fat reflection in the mirror. That would push me into a severe depression. Talking about being fat ... what's for eating?

BOTTLE MAN: A COMEDY | *Elena Naskova*

[MURIEL *gets up and heads toward the exit. She stops by the trash-can and takes the bottle out. She tries to look inside*]

MURIEL: Empty. Just like this place, and my life.

[MURIEL *smells the bottle*]

MURIEL: Is this how emptiness smells? [*Pause*] What did this bottle contain? Poison maybe. Maybe someone drank the poison. Maybe it was Romeo. Or Julia. [MURIEL *examines the bottle again*] Maybe if I washed it ... and what? Put some poison in it and drink it?

[MURIEL *pulls out the cork from the bottle with her teeth. The light starts to flicker and it goes off. When the light goes back on,* MAN *is standing at some distance from her. He's dressed in baggy light blue, satin pants and a long, light blue satin shirt.* MURIEL, *who still has the cork in her mouth, spits it out. The cork falls by* MAN'S *feet*]

MAN: What can I do for you, Master?

[MURIEL *screams*]

MAN: What can I do for you, Master?!

[MURIEL *throws the bottle at him. She misses*]

MAN: Don't break the bottle, Master. I'll be homeless if you break it.

MURIEL: Stay where you are, or I'm calling 911!

[MURIEL *rummages through her bag*]

MURIEL: Where's my cell phone?!

MAN: If you want me to go, Master, just close the bottle and I'll disappear.

MURIEL: The bottle! Where is the bottle?

[MURIEL *searches frantically for the bottle*]

MURIEL [*as she finds the bottle and picks it up*]: What do I close it with?

[MAN *bends and picks up the cork and offers it to* MURIEL. MURIEL *closes the bottle. The light flickers and goes off. When the light comes back,* MAN *is gone. Pause.* MURIEL *collapses to the floor*]

MURIEL: What was this? Am I dreaming or hallucinating? I'm tired and hungry and I'm making things up ... [*pause*] I should eat something and go to bed ... He called me Master ... What's there to eat in this house?

[MURIEL *exits. Blackout*]

Scene 2

[MURIEL *enters, dressed in cheap cotton pajamas. She looks around the living room, making sure that no one's there. She approaches the trashcan and digs out the bottle.* MURIEL *hesitates before she pulls out the cork. The light flickers and goes off. When the light comes fully on,* MAN *appears*]

MAN: What can I do for you, Master?

[MURIEL *quickly puts the cork back and* MAN *is gone*]

MURIEL: Shit! He's still here. Now what?

[MURIEL *stumbles to the sofa and sits down*]

MURIEL: I should call someone? I may be sick. [*Pause*] Yeah, but who? Ginger is out of town. Who else can I call?

[*Pause.* MURIEL *grabs the bottle and quickly opens it. The light flickers and goes off. When the light goes back on again,* MAN *is in the room*]

MAN: What can I do for you, Master?

MURIEL: How did you get into my apartment? I always lock the door.

MAN: It's not the door that I came through, Master. It's the bottle.

MURIEL: The bottle was empty. I tripped on it and almost fell, so I picked it up. What was the bottle doing on the street? I've been walking in that neighborhood for years and I've never, ever seen any garbage on the streets ... Except for, maybe, dog poop, sometimes. Hello? It's "Golden Hills" we're talking about. The best neighborhood in town.

MAN: Well, the bottle is yours now, Master. And so am I. What do you want me to do for you, Master?

MURIEL [*she checks him out*]: You want to do something for me?

MAN: I'm here to serve you, Master.

MURIEL [*she laughs, nervously*]: Are you expecting me to take you seriously?

MAN: Please do, Master. Please take me seriously. [*Pause*] What can I do for you, Master?

MURIEL: How am I supposed to use it ... you? Is there an instruction manual that comes with your bottle?

MAN: Just tell me what you wish, Master, and leave the rest to me.

MURIEL: And your name must be Genie.

BOTTLE MAN: A COMEDY | *Elena Naskova*

MAN: I am your Faithful Servant, Master.

MURIEL: Not Genie.

MAN: Genies are not real.

MURIEL: And you are?

MAN: I'm your Faithful Servant, Master. Just tell me what you want me to do for you.

MURIEL: What do you want to do for me?

MAN: Whatever you ask me to, Master. I'll do everything and anything to my ability.

MURIEL: So, it isn't anything?

MAN: Try me, Master.

MURIEL: Try you. What do you mean, "try you"?! [*Giggles*] Okay.

[MURIEL *finds a photo on her phone and shows it to* MAN]

MURIEL: Can you get me this?

MAN: A house?

MURIEL: The Courtly Mansion. It's in Golden Hills. I found you right in front of the Courtly Mansion ... I mean your bottle. And ... that's my dream house ... get it for me!

MAN: Is it for sale?

MURIEL: For sale? I don't think so and I don't care. Just get it for me.

MAN: Is the place already occupied, Master?

MURIEL: Of course it is! A fifty-something Blondie, with two large dogs. She likes to walk them around lunch time. I've tried to tell her "hello" a couple of times, but she avoids eye contact. There's probably a Mr. Blondie too, but I've never seen him. He must be working. Someone has to pay for that monster of house. Unless they had a bottle with someone like you.

MAN: If the house is occupied, Master, I don't think I can ...

MURIEL: Didn't you ask me what I wanted? That's what I want. What I really, really want.

MAN: It's not right to take someone's home.

MURIEL: Banks do it! Do you know what, Bottle Man? I have no use for you. So go back where you came from! [*Pause*] So what can you do for me? Can you at least do coffee? I want some coffee, can you at least get me some coffee, please?!

[MAN *lifts his hand. The light flickers, goes off and comes back on to reveal* MAN *holding a cup of coffee*]

Elena Naskova | BOTTLE MAN: A COMEDY

MURIEL: Oh, here you are. I thought that you were about to disappear. Why did the light turn off?
[MAN *puts the coffee in front of* MURIEL]
MAN: I perform better in the dark.
MURIEL: Perform? It's just a coffee. And it's black. [MURIEL *picks up the coffee and she drinks*] And it's bitter.
MAN: It's coffee.
MURIEL: One sugar, one cream. I take one sugar, one cream.
MAN: You didn't say that, Master.
MURIEL: Shouldn't you know that?
MAN: I can't read minds, Master. I'm sorry.
MURIEL: What else you can't do? I'm hungry, can you help me with that?
MAN: Most certainly, Master. What would you like?
MURIEL: I want an omelet.
MAN: What do you want in your omelet, Master?
MURIEL: Look, If I have to tell you everything, I better do it myself! Okay. Two eggs with three pieces of cheese and three pieces of bacon. I want it well done. I want some toast, too. Two pieces of toast. And please, please, please don't burn my toast. I hate that.
MAN: Omelet coming right away, Master.
[*The light flickers and goes off. When the light comes on,* MAN *is holding a tray with breakfast. He puts the tray in front of* MURIEL]
MURIEL: That looks good. It smells good, too. Thank you! [MURIEL *takes a bite*] Yum. Pretty good. Eat with me.
MAN: Eating is not an activity I'm equipped to perform, Master.
MURIEL: That sucks, Bottle Man. Because, you should be equipped to perform whatever I ask you to.
MAN: I'm sorry, Master, but I have my limitations.
MURIEL: You sure do, don't you? The thing is, Mr. Bottle Man, you're a man … A big man, a strong man … and you say, you're my servant. My "faithful servant," mind you. What I'm … what I'm trying to say is that … you shouldn't create false expectations. Because, I hate being disappointed. I've been disappointed again and again … and again! People always overpromise, underdeliver. Why do you think I don't have a boyfriend? And

BOTTLE MAN: A COMEDY | *Elena Naskova*

you're not "just people." you're supposed to be more than that. Do you see what I mean?

MAN: No, Master, I don't.

MURIEL: Forget it. You're not very bright, are you?

[MURIEL *opens one of the magazines and looks through it. She stops at a page*]

MURIEL: I love this, but I'm ... I'm ... if I was 20 pounds lighter ... [MURIEL *looks at* MAN] I know! Take 20 pounds off of me. I want to be 20 pounds lighter. So, do it! Make me 20 pounds lighter. Twenty or so, you can go up to 30 really, so I have some room to grow ... But, I can always ask you to do it again.

MAN: I'm very sorry, Master, but I'm not equipped to take. I can only give.

MURIEL: You would be giving, Dodo! Giving by taking. Understand?

MAN: Taking isn't giving, Master.

MURIEL: But it is! It can be! Giving can be taking and taking can be giving!

MAN: Sorry Master, but I'm only equipped to give by giving.

[MURIEL *angrily leafs through the magazine*]

MURIEL: This is what I want. Double-fleece robe. The red one.

MAN: Is that a request, Master?

[MURIEL *turns another page and shows it to* MAN]

MURIEL: Come here and look at this Kingfield sweater. The red one. I love red. There were some boots I really liked too, I had marked them ... Here. See? And these stone-wash jeans.

MAN: I have a hard time following you, Master.

MURIEL: I'm making a list for you. Look at this dress! I could wear this dress for the Christmas party. The office Christmas party that I wasn't going to attend, because I didn't have a date! But now that you showed up, find me a date! Find me someone to go to the Christmas party with. [*Pause*] Hello?! I'm talking to you. Find me a man to accompany me to the party.

MAN: A living man?

MURIEL: What would I do with a dead one? I need him alive while at the party. And not just "alive," but nice looking, too ... someone around my age, six feet or taller ... intelligent ... it would be nice if I could choose from a few ... options ...

MAN: A living man has a free will, Master.

MURIEL: So?

MAN: A living man is free to do whatever he chooses to.

MURIEL: Okay, whatever! I want a man that'll chose to accompany me to my office Christmas party!

MAN: Why don't you find him yourself, Master?

MURIEL: Because I can't! For some crazy, unexplainable reason, men don't choose to be with me. If I could find me a man why would bother asking you? [*Pause.* MURIEL *stares at* MAN] Or maybe, I *can* find me a man for the Christmas party ...

[*Blackout*]

Scene 3

[MURIEL's *living room, night. There are new clothes, shoes, and various other objects all over the room.* MURIEL *enters. She is dressed in a double-fleece robe, and new silk pajamas. She starts looking for the bottle*]

MURIEL [*finding the bottle*]: Here you are! [MURIEL *opens the cork, the light flickers, goes off and when it goes back on,* MAN *appears*]

MAN: What can I do for you, Master?

MURIEL: I can't sleep. Sit down with me and keep me company.

[MAN *sits down.* MURIEL *moves closer to him*]

MURIEL: I'm getting really excited ... about the Christmas party, this Sunday. I think you'll do just fine. Better than any other idiot that will be there.

MAN: Thank you for believing in me, Master.

MURIEL: Believing ... believe ... believing. Seems like it's your favorite word! What does believe even mean? What I believe, Bottle Man, is that belief is irrelevant. Something is true or false, regardless whether you believe or not. What do you think about that?

MAN: If that's what you believe, Master, then that must be true ... for you.

MURIEL: I'm just messing with you, Bottle Man. Do you know what I really like about you? I like it how ... you appear and disappear, depending on whether I chose to open, or to close the bottle. I wish I could do that with other people. [*Pause*] I bet that the person who had you before me, misses you a lot. Do you miss her?

BOTTLE MAN: A COMEDY | *Elena Naskova*

MAN: Who, Master?

MURIEL: Who had you before me?

MAN: I only know of you, Master.

MURIEL: Was it the Blondie with the two big dogs? The one that lives in my mansion, and you can't kick her out? Was she your previous owner? Did she lose you, or did she throw you out? Maybe you didn't meet her expectations? [*Pause*] Don't you remember anything?!

MAN: I'm not equipped to remember, Master.

MURIEL: Wouldn't that be great?! I wish I wasn't equipped to remember some things ... I lot actually ... [*Pause*] Well, just so you know, I'll never throw you away, Bottle Man. I'm just not that type of a person. You can see it for yourself, I keep all kinds of shit.

MAN: Thank you, Master. That's very kind of you.

MURIEL: And also ... I don't want to call you Bottle Man anymore. It sounds kind of ... common.

MAN: I don't mind it, Master.

MURIEL: How about ... Anthony ... no ... wait, I had an ex called Anthony. He was a jerk. How about ... Robert ... no ... no Robert. How about, Walter? I like Walter. [*Pause*] Hey Walter, can you do something about your outfit? You look ridiculous in those blue pants. Okay, Walter? Change your outfit. Please?

MAN: What should I wear, Master?

MURIEL: Well ... How about a gray sports suit and a ... wait a second ...

[MURIEL *searches for a magazine. She finds it, opens it and looks through it. She stops at a page and shows it to* MAN]

MURIEL: I want you to wear something like this. And do something about your hair, please. You can use a shave, too. That two-day beard is not you.

[MAN *is about to lift his hand*]

MURIEL: Wait! And wear some Versace L'Homme perfume on you. Not too much. Only a drop, or two. [*Pause*] All right. That'll do it for now. Walter, it's a request!

[MAN *lifts his hand. The light flickers and goes off.* MAN *disappears. Pause*]

MURIEL: Walter! Walter ... Is it something I said? [*Pause*] I started believing it's for real. I'm so naïve.

[*Pause. The light goes on.* MAN *enters, dressed in a sports suit.* MURIEL *stares at him*]

MAN: What can I do for you Master?

MURIEL: Wow, Walter. [*Pause*] Walter, I never asked you ... are you ... solid? [*Pause*] Never mind, I'll check it out myself.

[MURIEL *gets up and approaches him, seductively. Music starts.* MURIEL *touches his arm, hesitantly*]

MURIEL: Walter, do you believe in metamorphosis?

MAN: I don't know, Master. I'm not sure.

MURIEL: There is still a lot of work to be done on you, but ... it can be accomplished. You have potential, and you're in good hands.

[MURIEL *takes the* MAN's *other hand and she starts dancing.* MAN *tries to follow. They dance until* MAN *steps on* MURIEL's *feet and stops dancing.* MURIEL *laughs and sits back down*]

MURIEL: My poor foot! You're little clumsy, but not too bad.

MAN: I apologize, Master. I'm sorry. I'm not very good at this.

MURIEL: You'll get there, Walter. I believe in you.

[MURIEL *takes the bottle*]

MURIEL: You know Walter. I take back what I said about believing. I believe that you're for real, and that's the truth. [*Looks at the bottle*] I don't think, I need this, anymore.

[MURIEL *is about to throw the bottle against the wall, but then she changes her mind*]

MURIEL [*continuing*]: I'll keep it. Just for when I want to be alone.

THE END

Шишко: Комедија

Ликови

МАРИЈА: околу четириесет години
ШИШКО: триесетина години.

BOTTLE MAN: A COMEDY | Elena Naskova

Поставување

Станот на МАРИЈА со кауч, масичка, канта за ѓубре, и расфрлани алишта и модни каталози по подот.

Сцена 1

[МАРИЈА влегува, си ја фрла ташната на каучот, седнува, си ги соблекува чевлите и си ги масира стапалата]

МАРИЈА: Овие чевли ќе ме стават во инвалидска количка.

[МАРИЈА си ги соблекува чорапите, ги помирисува и се мршти. Ги фрла чорапите на под]

МАРИЈА: Токсичен отпадок. Може и да експлодира.

[МАРИЈА си ги става нозете на масичката, и вади едно шише од ташната. Го разгледува шишето и се обидува да го исчисти со ракав]

МАРИЈА: Сувенир, или парче ѓубре од Златниот Рид. И зошто го зедов со себе? Го собрав од земјата и го донесов тука, зошто?

[МАРИЈА го фрла шишето во кантата за ѓубре, зема еден каталог и го листа]

МАРИЈА: Види го пењоров колку е добар. А пижамиве? Свилени. Обожавам свила. И викаат свила била демоде. Свила не може никогаш да е демоде. Јас би купила две од овие. Ама од каде пари?

[МАРИЈА го фрла каталогот]

МАРИЈА: Пак се занесувам. Ама и зошто ќе ми се? Кој ќе ме гледа во свилени пижами? На кој му е гајле што носам во кревет? Можам слободно да си се шетам и гола по дома. Ама, само во темница. Да не се видам случајно во огледало па да паднам во тешка депресија. (пауза) Ептен се здебелив оваа година ... ама еве и сега ми се јаде. А да идам да видам што имам за јадење?

[МАРИЈА се упатува кон кујната, застанува пред кантата за ѓубре, ја отвара и го вади шишето. Го анализира]

МАРИЈА: Празно е. Исто како ... исто како овој стан и како ... исто како мојот живот.

[Го помирисува шишето]

МАРИЈА: Чудно мириса. Вака ли мириса празнината? [*Пауза*] Што ли имало во ова шише? Можеби отров. Можеби некој го испил и ... Можеби бил Ромео. Или Јулија? [*Пак го разгледува шишето*] Можеби ако го измијам ... И да го измијам и што? Да си ставам отров и да си го испијам?

[*МАРИЈА ја вади тапата од шишето. Светлото почнува да трепери и се гаси. Кога светлото повторно се пали, МАРИЈА не е сама во собата. Во собата е и ШИШКО, облечен во сини, свилени панталони и сина, свилена блуза. Стаписана, МАРИЈА ја испушта тапата од раце*]

ШИШКО: Што би сакале од мене, Газда?

[*МАРИЈА вришти*]

ШИШКО: Во ред ли сте, Газда!

[*МАРИЈА го фрла шишето кон ШИШКО. Го промашува*]

The Bra Bust

Joyce Newman Scott

Cast

ANNIE: 50–60 years old, widowed. Former beauty who has lost touch with her inner beauty. Feeling invisible

COLLEEN: 50–60 years old, sometimes snarky, but faithful best friend to ANNIE

BELINDA: forties, a confident, elegant trans woman, slightly over the top. In casting, think of the TV series *Pose*.

Time

The present.

Setting

A dressing room in an upscale store.

COLLEEN [*into phone*]: no, they didn't tell us why. We were having lunch in Neiman's ... and they just told us the store was in lockdown. Honey, it's probably a false alarm. You know how shaky the world is right now ... right ... right ... yes. Everyone's on the verge of hysteria. [*Critically studies* ANNIE] She's fine. No, really! She's fine. Well sorta?

ANNIE [*while taking a bra off a hanger, she yells over her shoulder*]: Tell him we had a choice of staying and drinking ... or shopping. You wanted to drink ... I needed a new bra. My strap broke when I dove under the table. I think that waiter overreacted.

COLLEEN [*to* ANNIE]: We would still be drinking if you hadn't gotten us kicked out of the restaurant. [*To phone*] See, there was this loud noise when one of the Christmas displays fell over and took down a six-foot tree.

ANNIE [*defensively*]: I was simply trying to evacuate the restaurant in an organized manner.

COLLEEN: You crawled under the table and screamed "Run for your lives." You caused a stampede. That poor waiter who got trampled may never recover.

ANNIE: My training is to evacuate quickly. On an airplane you have one second per person. My old method was to yell "follow me," and *voilà*.

COLLEEN: That only works when you're in your twenties. In your sixties you become invisible.

ANNIE: I know. So, I improvised.

COLLEEN [*listening into the phone*]: Harold wants to know how much we had?

ANNIE [*yells from across the room*]: Don't worry. We're sober. I only took a Xanax, to help my migraine ...

COLLEEN: Followed by two Margaritas.

ANNIE [*slurs slightly*]: Three ... to be exact ... ly. And my migraine is gone ... almost.

COLLEEN [*giggles into the phone*]: Without salt. Cause we are watching our blood pressure. [ANNIE *holds up several bras trying to decide which one to try on*]

ANNIE: What do you think? Off-white or flesh-toned?

COLLEEN: You're not decorating the Statue of Liberty. Either. No one ever sees it. You live in baggy pants and T-shirts 24/7.

ANNIE: They're comfy. Look, I've lived in a uniform my whole life. I went to a Catholic school then I became a flight attendant. I don't coordinate colors well.

COLLEEN: But you used to. When Fred was alive.

ANNIE [*sighs, reflectively*]: I know ... I was hot back then. But I had a reason.

[*There's a knock on the door and* BELINDA *enters. She's a stunning black trans woman dressed in a classic two-piece form fitting tweed suit, with big hair and false eyelashes. She is charmingly over the top*]

BELINDA [*in a lilting saleslady voice*]: Ladies ... I've got *beaucoup* presents.

COLLEEN: [*shocked and taken aback*]: You definitely have the wrong room.

BELINDA: I'm your saleslady.

THE BRA BUST | Joyce Newman Scott

COLLEEN: What happened to Laura? I've always worked with Laura.

BELINDA: She quit when some idiot set off a panic alarm in the restaurant. But don't worry ladies, I'm the new department manager, and I'm here to bring you great service. [BELINDA *hangs several brightly colored bras on the rack and pulls out a tape measure. She moves toward* ANNIE]

ANNIE: Whoa. What are you doing?

BELINDA: I took a wild guess. Now let's see what bra size you really are, sweetheart. Don't worry. I won't bite. Belinda's here to help you spice up your lives.

ANNIE [*horrified*]: I've been wearing the same size 36C for years. In beige. No lace. No padding. No frills. No fuss.

BELINDA: Most women wear the wrong size bra most of their lives and never even know it.

COLLEEN: He's right. I read that in *Cosmo* … or was it *Vogue*?

ANNIE: Good point. [*Beat*] Why is a man working in ladies apparel?

BELINDA: She. I'm a she. I identify as a woman.

ANNIE: But you're …

BELINDA: An elegant woman with amazing style.

COLLEEN: I think I'm going to pass out.

ANNIE: Don't you dare leave me alone.

COLLEEN: And miss all this action? Wouldn't dream of it.

BELINDA [*looking at Annie's breasts*]: Those poor babies need some lift and love. Bet you haven't seen a padded push-up lace bra since high school.

COLLEEN: She's right. Your girls *are* drooping.

ANNIE [*to Colleen*]: Who's side are you on, anyway?

COLLEEN: Yours … His … Her's … I'm not sure, yet. I'm confused. [*She remembers* HAROLD's *still on the cell phone*] I'll call you back. We have a situation … No, calm down … we're not evacuating. This time, we have a bra emergency. [*She clicks her phone then tosses it in her purse*]

ANNIE [*to Belinda*]: I like my bras plain. And my gravity is just where it should be at my age. We'll call if we need you. Good bye.

BELINDA: I can't abandon a client who is obviously in a wardrobe crisis.

Joyce Newman Scott | THE BRA BUST

COLLEEN: What does that mean?

BELINDA [*referring to the drab bras*]: I mean look at your choices. Lord help us.

ANNIE: Thank you very much. Now, go. [*BELINDA doesn't budge. She blocks the door*]

COLLEEN: I think my migraine is coming back.

BELINDA: I'm a certified measurer. And I'm good at my job. Last year I sold Dolly Parton a La Perla push-up bra with sequins. Now, she calls me monthly for advice and we discuss her music projects.

COLLEEN [*to ANNIE*]: Oh, I loved *9 to 5*. And she has much bigger boobs than you do.

ANNIE [*to COLLEEN*]: Pick a team, Colleen.

[*COLLEEN flops down onto a padded chair*]

COLLEEN: But she knows Dolly. What harm can it do?

BELINDA: What are you afraid of? We're not just a wee bit prejudiced, are we?

COLLEEN: Heck no. Some of my best friends are black.

ANNIE: Zip it, Colleen.

BELINDA: And how many are trans?

COLLEEN: Okay, you got me there.

BELINDA [*to ANNIE*]: What I see is a gorgeous woman in her sexual prime who's hiding her best assets.

ANNIE: Gorgeous? Really? Go on!

COLLEEN [*not willing to let go*]: I am not biased. I was on the anti-defamation committee in high school. [*BELINDA and ANNIE ignore COLLEEN as she rambles*]

ANNIE [*suddenly getting weepy*]: I mean look at me. It's hopeless. I'm old. People look past me, not at me.

BELINDA: Honey, don't get maudlin, but you're singing my song.

ANNIE: You have no idea what it feels like to be in an aging body.

BELINDA [*there's a long pause*]: You're kidding, right? I know what it feels like to be in the wrong body. That count?

COLLEEN [*to ANNIE*]: Fred's gone. You're still here.

BELINDA: Sweetie. You can upgrade. You know ... rebuild the chassis and soup up the motor. A new coat of paint. And pretty soon you're flying down that highway doing 140. Now you got a Ferrari where there used to be a Volkswagen.

THE BRA BUST | *Joyce Newman Scott*

COLLEEN: She's right. You need a radical change. Since Fred died, life is passing you by.

BELINDA: You need to create a new persona.

ANNIE: I agree with you. Wait a minute. Am I taking bra advice from a transvestite?

BELINDA: I'm trans gender, sweetheart. A transvestite dresses like a woman. A trans person chooses to live as her true self. And I'm horrified you don't know the difference. Let's be honest, OK. There's very little difference between us. Society manufactures our persona. It starts as children. Who says you have to keep what you got?

ANNIE: Persona?

BELINDA: Yes, an individual's social facade or front ... A sponge. It's Jung.

COLLEEN: What?

BELINDA: I've spent a lot of time with my therapist. [*Points to her own body*] This doesn't happen overnight.

ANNIE: I believe in working with what nature gave me.

BELINDA: So do I ... But like an ill-fitting bra sometimes nature needs an upgrade.

ANNIE: I believe in nature taking its course.

COLLEEN [*coughs, to interrupt* ANNIE]: Didn't you have a face lift ... ?

ANNIE: Fifteen years ago. Back then I was more superficial. I've evolved since then.

COLLEEN: Yes, and your evolution is making you ... boring. That's the problem. Since Fred died. A piece of you has gone underground.

ANNIE: Why do I feel like this is a friggin' intervention?

BELINDA: There's a fabulous figure under those ... whatever they are ... pajamas? [BELINDA *piles* ANNIE'*s hair up on top of her head*]

BELINDA: Now visualize yourself in a low-cut V-neck, tight jeans, a pair of knee boots, a cool hip leather jacket.

ANNIE: I'm vegan. I don't do leather.

BELINDA: Okay, Jeans, jacket. With studs. We got star quality here. Why are you hiding it? [ANNIE *gazes at herself in the mirror. She starts to accept the new image*]

ANNIE: I still do look hot ... kinda.

BELINDA: I'm stepping outside while you try on that Ferrari.

ANNIE: Belinda?

BELINDA: Yes.

ANNIE: Show me that La Perla with the sequins that Dolly bought? I think I'm ready to come out of mourning.

BELINDA: I'd love to. [*COLLEEN's cell phone rings, she fishes it out of her purse. She sees it's HAROLD*]

COLLEEN [*to HAROLD*]: Hi honey, plan on making dinner for yourself, okay? I have a feeling we're going to be a while. [*Beat*] What are we doing ... ?

ANNIE [*unhooks a bra from its hanger and yells over her shoulder*]: We're upgrading the chassis. Then the ladies are all going out for drinks. [*To Belinda*] The three of us, right?

COLLEEN: Make that three Margaritas. With salt. Screw the blood pressure.

BELINDA: Ladies, I'd be delighted.

ANNIE: That waiter is really going to be surprised to see us, again!

BELINDA: Tell him "The Bra Bust Ladies" are on their way!

THE END

O Sutiã

Em um camarim numa loja de departamentos de lux, COLLEEN e ANNIE entram carregando vários sutiãs beige. Colleen está falando com seu marido HAROLD em seu celular. Ambas as mulheres estão ligeiramente embriagadas.

COLLEEN [*ao telefone*]: Não, eles não nos disseram o porquê. Estávamos almoçando no Neiman's ... e eles nos disseram que a loja estava fechada. Querida, provavelmente é um alarme falso. Você sabe como o mundo está instável agora ... certo ... certo ... sim. Todos estão à beira da histeria." [*Criticamente, estuda Annie*] "Ela está bem. Não mesmo! Ela está bem. Tipo?

ANNIE [*enquanto tira um sutiã do cabide, ela grita por cima do ombro*]: Diga-lhe que escolhemos ficar e beber ... ou fazer compras. Você queria beber ... Eu precisava de um sutiã novo. Minha alça quebrou quando mergulhei debaixo da mesa. Acho que o garçom exagerou.

COLLEEN [*para Aninha*]: Ainda estaríamos bebendo se você não tivesse nos expulsado do restaurante. [*Para HAROLD no telefone*] Veja, houve um barulho alto quando uma das exibições de Natal caiu e derrubou uma árvore de 1,80m.

ANNIE [*defensivamente*]: Eu estava simplesmente tentando sair do restaurante de maneira organizada.

COLLEEN: Você se arrastou para debaixo da mesa e gritou "Corram pelas suas vidas". Você causou uma debandada. Aquele pobre garçom que foi pisoteado pode nunca se recuperar.

ANNIE: Meu treinamento é sair rapidamente. Em um avião você tem um segundo por pessoa. Meu antigo método era gritar "sigam-me" e pronto.

COLLEEN: Isso só funciona quando você está na casa dos vinte. Em seus sessenta anos você se torna invisível.

ANNIE: Eu sei. Então, eu improvisei.

COLLEEN [*ouvindo no telefone*]: Harold quer saber quanto nós tínhamos?

ANNIE [*grita do outro lado da sala*]: Não se preocupe. Estamos sóbrias. Eu só tomei um Xanax, para ajudar na minha enxaqueca ...

COLLEEN: Seguido por duas Margaritas.

ANNIE [*reclama levemente*]: Três ... para ser exatamente ... exatamente. E minha enxaqueca se foi ... pelo menos.

COLLEEN [*ri ao telefone*]: Sem sal. Porque estamos observando nossa pressão arterial.

[*ANNIE segura vários sutiãs tentando decidir qual experimentar*]

ANNIE: O que você acha? Branco ou tom de pele?

COLLEEN: Você não está decorando a Estátua da Liberdade. Qualquer um. Ninguém nunca vai ver. Você vive em calças largas e camisetas 24 horas por dia, 7 dias por semana.

ANNIE: Eles são confortáveis. Olha, eu vivi de uniforme toda a minha vida. Fui para uma escola católica e depois tornei-me comissária de bordo. Não coordeno bem as cores.

COLLEEN: Mas você costumava. Quando Fred estava vivo.

ANNIE [*suspira, reflexivamente*]: Eu sei ... eu era gostoso naquela época. Mas eu tinha um motivo. [*Nesse momento, há uma batida* na porta e BELINDA entra. Ela é uma mulher trans negra deslumbrante (40 e poucos anos) vestida com um terno clássico de duas peças, com cabelos grandes e cílios postiços. Ela está encantadoramente por cima]

BELINDA [com uma voz melodiosa de vendedora]: "Senhoras ... Tenho presentes lindos."

COLLEEN [chocado e surpreso]: Você definitivamente está no quarto errado.

BELINDA: Eu sou sua vendedora.

COLLEEN: O que aconteceu com Laurinha? Sempre trabalhei com a Laura.

BELINDA: Ela desistiu quando alguma pessoa idiota disparou um alarme de pânico no restaurante. Mas não se preocupem, senhoras, sou o novo gerente de departamento e estou aqui para oferecer um ótimo serviço."

[BELINDA pendura vários sutiãs coloridos no cabide e tira uma fita métrica. Ela se move em direção a ANNIE]

ANNIE: Uau. O que você está fazendo?

BELINDA: Eu dei um palpite. Agora vamos ver que tamanho de sutiã você realmente é, querida. Não se preocupe. não vou te morder. Belinda está aqui para ajudá-los a apimentar suas vidas.

ANNIE [horrorizado]: Eu uso o mesmo tamanho 36C, faz anos. Em beige. Sem renda. Sem preenchimento. Sem frescuras. Sem confusões.

What Comes After Sorrow

Ornella Ohayon

Cast

VIA: 25 years old, the protagonist
MOTHER: fifties, VIA's mother
DAD: fifties, VIA's father
SISTER: thirties, VIA's sister
BROTHER: 29 years old, VIA's brother
FRANK: thirties, VIA's sister's fiancé
EX-BOYFRIEND: 28 years old, VIA's ex-boyfriend.

Setting

A family dinner, somewhere in the world.

Time

Evening.

Act 1

VIA: So due to recent events I've had to give up my apartment and move back home with my mother. Which has been … lovely. [*Beat*] She's a nice woman my mother. Mostly says things like:

MOTHER: You're so pretty when you put the right clothes on.

VIA: And she means it in a good way, so I can't get mad at her and tell her that really it just means without clothes I am unattractive, which is something I'm sure my ex-boyfriend would disagree with because he seemed to particularly enjoy my company when I didn't have any clothes on. [*Beat*] Anyway. [*Beat*] I've been trying to get my life back together ever since, interviewing for pretty useless jobs so that I can get myself a very useful apartment.

[*DAD sneezes*]

My dad is also in the house. With my mother. They have separate rooms though and he sleeps in the smallest room of the house.

Not a smaller room, the *smallest* of the house. In a house full of rooms. Which brings me to say things like I've moved back with my mother and not realize I've actually moved back with both my parents. [*Beat*] A dreary guy my dad. He mostly says things like:

DAD: With this brain of yours you could have done something with yourself.

VIA: Which is a lovely thing to say, really, if you know my dad. [*Whispers*] Don't feel bad that you don't. [*Beat*] He means well. He's trying to tell me that I'm smart. He doesn't know he's also saying I fucked up my life, because then he'd realize it kinda invalidates what he's saying in the first place. 'Cause if you fuck up your life despite having been blessed with great intelligence then really, you're just plain stupid.

[EX-BOYFRIEND *enters. He walks up next to* VIA]

VIA: My ex was stupid. The smart kind of stupid. That's a great thing to have. It's the kind that makes you able to bear going to parties *and* talking to the people who attend them.

[EX-BOYFRIEND *mimes filming a movie enthusiastically*]

He's a self-taught movie producer, which is the kind of job that makes you talk to people you don't know and say things like:

EX-BOYFRIEND: Your script sounds amazing, give my assistant a call on Monday she'll schedule something.

VIA: He doesn't have an assistant.

[EX-BOYFRIEND *walks off*]

VIA [*showing her party dress*]: Probably wondering what that is. Sister's engagement dinner tonight. I usually avoid family reunions the only way I can – by moving across the country – but yesterday I got some amazing news that might actually solve all my problems and give my existence some meaning. So I decided I might attend. [*Beat*] Plus it's my sister's engagement dinner. It's a rebound marriage. I know right? Two words that do not go together. But my sister's the kind of smart that shows by big diplomas and professional accomplishment so the fact that she is unable to stay alone for longer than one fucking minute is something everyone chooses to overlook. [*Beat*] She often says things like:

SISTER: Really you should thank me.

WHAT COMES AFTER SORROW | Ornella Ohayon

VIA: And when I say "why?" she tends to say things like:
SISTER: At least my divorce got them off your back for a bit.
VIA: She got divorced three months ago. We figured they just had a difference of opinion, but it turns out they actually had one very similar interest. Dudes. [Beat] She's pretty even with the wrong clothes on and when she announced her new engagement before her divorce was even finalized we were all really thrown, so we threw *her* an engagement dinner party. [Beat] And while everyone was busy being devastated about my sister's divorce and I was *finally* getting a very much needed break from being a 25-year-old unemployed young woman who had to move back home, my sister was busy getting F ... –
MOTHER: Frank!
[*A handsome man enters. It is FRANK*]
VIA: Frank. She was busy getting FFF ... Frank. [Beat] Frank's handsome.
[*FRANK demonstrates his handsomeness to the audience by doing a little comb-my-hair fix-my-tie combo then sits quietly next to SISTER*]
[*MOTHER gets up to admire VIA's dress. Picks it up a bit*]
MOTHER: See? Lovely. Now if you wore things like this a bit more often –
[*BROTHER enters*]
BROTHER: Mom! You look beautiful.
MOTHER: Darling!
[*They hug*]
VIA: My brother's a life saver.
[*BROTHER winks at the audience. He and MOTHER go sit on the couch*]
But also like, literally. [Beat] He's a neonatal surgeon. Which means he not only saves lives, he saves tiny little baby lives. [Beat] He calls me sweet pie which would actually be nice, if he hadn't been calling me that since I was twelve for the sole reason I once puked all over the table at a Friday night dinner because I ate too much pie.
[*Everyone sitting on the couch gets up and takes a seat at the dinner table*]

MOTHER: Where is your sister? Late as always. [*She calls for* VIA] Olivia?!
VIA: I'm not a fan of my name. Always found it so ... dramatic.
BROTHER: Even when she lives at home she still finds a way to be late to dinners.
SISTER: I'll go get her. [SISTER *gets up and joins* VIA *at the front of the stage*] I need to talk to you.
[VIA *looks at her, then at the audience, then back at her*]
VIA [*to* SISTER]: I'm a little busy right now.
SISTER: It's important.
VIA [*to audience*]: This actually happens quite often. [*To* SISTER] Okay. [*Beat*] I know what you're gonna say and I'm sorry if I may have seemed unsupportive about your super sudden wedding but I've wrapped my mind around it now and I promise you that me and my very uncomfortable dress 100 percent support you.
SISTER: I can't get married.
VIA: *I knew it.*
[VIA *starts to take off her dress rapidly.* SISTER *attempts to stop her*]
SISTER: Don't! Please now is not the time to be dramatic!
VIA [*still trying to take it off*]: If you all didn't want me to be dramatic you shouldn't have named me – [*very dramatically*] Olivia.
[*They struggle. It's a mess*]
SISTER: I am not the one who named you. Will you stop –
[VIA *stops. They both stare at each other, out of breath.* VIA *glances at the audience*]
VIA [*to audience*]: I'm cool. [*To* SISTER] I'm cool.
SISTER: Frank is great I mean he's funny he's handsome. I just. I just don't ...
VIA: Love him.
SISTER [*emotional*]: What's wrong with me?
VIA: Nothing! Nothing.
[*Beat*]
SISTER: You're gonna help me, right?
VIA [*to audience*]: The good thing about majoring in playwriting is that people always think you can come up with some super creative way to solve all their problems. [*To* SISTER] Just pull him aside and tell him so I can get out of this *ridiculous dress* please.

WHAT COMES AFTER SORROW | *Ornella Ohayon*

SISTER: No, I can't tell him tonight I can't. I can't face Mom. You know how she gets.
[*VIA glances at the audience*]
VIA: No. How does she get?
[*SISTER scoffs*]
VIA: Kidding. Jeez okay. Just rip off the Band-Aid, pull him aside, let him off easy. And once he takes off I can smooth things over with some pretty amazing news I just got.
SISTER: New job?
VIA: No.
SISTER: Boyfriend?
VIA: Nope.
SISTER: Negative pregnancy test?
VIA: Yes, but not telling Mom *that*.
[*BROTHER gets up and joins them at the front of the stage*]
BROTHER: Guys. What the fuck? We're all waiting for you. I'm starving!
VIA [*to SISTER*]: Just rip off –
SISTER: The Band-Aid.
[*Both sisters share a look and SISTER walks towards the table*]
VIA [*to audience*]: Never gonna do it.
[*SISTER just stands in front of the table for a second and ... sits*]
VIA [*to SISTER*]: Knew you could do ... it proud of you! [*To BROTHER*] Okay let's go eat.
[*VIA goes and sits at the table when BROTHER's phone rings. He takes the call*]
BROTHER [*on the phone*]: Yeah. What? [*Beat*] Wait, what? You said it was a sure win!
[*VIA gets up from the table and walks towards him*]
BROTHER: You're telling me I lost all of it? [*Noticing her*] I'll call you back. Just ... fix it okay!
VIA [*to audience*]: Gambling problem. [*To BROTHER*] Problem?
BROTHER: No, no, everything is fine. [*Beat*] Actually. Do you think you can ask Dad for your bat mitzvah money?
VIA: What?
BROTHER: I know you hate asking for money but you're the only one who still has money on Dad's account so –
VIA: So I'm asking Dad for my money and then give it to you?

BROTHER: I promise you I will pay you back every cent.
VIA [*to audience*]: I'll just keep pretending I am shocked for a bit before I eventually agree to ask for the money. [*Absolutely shocked to* BROTHER] You're a surgeon how do you not have enough –
BROTHER: Look I swear it's nothing bad okay I just made a wrong investment –
VIA: It's bad enough that it keeps you from asking Dad for money yourself.
BROTHER: I *could* do it myself.
[VIA *glances at the audience*]
BROTHER: You're just … so much better at this than we are.
[VIA *glances at the audience*]
VIA [*to* BROTHER]: I could use that money to get out of here you know – it's been hell by the way thanks for asking … has that ever occurred to you?
BROTHER: So why didn't you use it already?
VIA [*to audience*]: Totally forgot about my bat mitzvah money. [*to* BROTHER] Because I knew you'd pull that crap again and you'd need me. Again.
BROTHER: But … You'll help me, right?
[VIA *glances at the audience*]
[*Everyone that was sitting at the table gets up, starts lifting the table, and carefully brings it over to the front of the stage near* VIA *and* BROTHER]
FRANK: We figured it'd be easier that way.
VIA [*to audience*]: Frank's handsome.
[*They all sit*]
MOTHER: Ah. All my children are here. God bless us!
[DAD *pours wine in everyone's glass.* VIA *gives him a quick look* "pour some more in mine." *He does*]
MOTHER: So! What is new with everyone?
VIA: Well, actually …
MOTHER [*to* BROTHER]: Any new baby saved this week honey?
BROTHER: There are new ones every day, ma'.
MOTHER: Of course darling that was a silly question.
VIA [*fake laughing*]: Then why do you ask it all the time? [*She drinks*]

WHAT COMES AFTER SORROW | *Ornella Ohayon*

BROTHER: Aw. Don't worry sweet pie you'll find a new job. All in good time. Right, Dad?
DAD: All in good time.
VIA: Right. Well it's funny you say that because it turns out ...
MOTHER [*to BROTHER*]: It *is* funny you say that darling thank you. [*To VIA*] Because we've all been talking actually and we think that maybe –
VIA: You've *all* been talking? Like, all of you.
MOTHER: Yes. And we all agreed that it could actually be a good idea for you to ... [*takes her time finding the words*] ... go back to school.
VIA: I went to school, Mom.
MOTHER: No, of course you did sweetie. [*To others*] Right?
EVERYONE ELSE: Yeah / Of course she did / Definitely.
MOTHER: We just thought if you went back to school then it could help to have an extra degree. Maybe this time you could major in something ... [*She takes her time finding the word*]
VIA [*to audience*]: Useful.
MOTHER: Else.
SISTER: My firm hires a lot of people with a political degree; they don't actually have to have gone to law school.
MOTHER: There you go!
VIA [*calmly*]: Well, I appreciate all of your opinions but I am not going back to school, thank you.
MOTHER: You could at least consider it.
VIA [*obviously sarcastic*]: This is nice. All of us together, not judging each other.
SISTER: You don't have to be like this you know –
VIA [*to audience*]: We're just trying to help you.
SISTER: We're just trying to ...
BROTHER: Help you. Sweet pie. Right?
EVERYONE ELSE: Right / Yeah / Definitely.
[*VIA raises her glass*]
VIA [*to SISTER and FRANK*]: You guys, congratulations again.
[*Everyone raises their glass except SISTER*]
DAD / MOTHER / BROTHER: Congratulations you guys.
VIA: So tell us about the wedding ... I mean do we have a date yet? A caterer? A place?

[SISTER *kicks* VIA *under the table. Hard*]
VIA [*through the pain*]: Worth it.
FRANK: Oh well we don't want to bore you with the details –
VIA: Please do. Bore us.
BROTHER: Any plans for a baby yet? 'Cause you know this one I can't help deliver!
[*Everyone laughs.* VIA *especially loud*]
SISTER: Definitely thinking about it.
MOTHER: Ooh lovely! As long as you don't wait for ten years to start trying. [*To* DAD] Like honey do you remember what happened to the Greenbergs? [*To everyone*] They thought they had all the time in the world, they traveled, tried all sorts of careers, and when they started trying ... bam. Wife couldn't get pregnant. [*To* DAD] Wasn't that awful honey?
DAD: Awful.
MOTHER: They ran all kinds of tests, inconclusive. Everyone thought well dammit that woman is just barren. Husband leaves her, bam. Out of the blue. [*To* DAD] It was awful for that woman, wasn't it honey?
DAD: Awful.
MOTHER: Two years later –
[VIA *chugs her glass of wine*]
MOTHER: He's finally remarried and you know, trying for a baby again, the poor guy.
VIA [*to audience*]: Poor guy.
MOTHER: Can you imagine what happens next?
[VIA *pours herself more wine*]
MOTHER: A year later still no baby. Now if I was him, I'd start thinking, you know, what could I have done in another life to be so unlucky that two of my wives are barren? So he decides to run some tests for himself.
VIA: Smart guy.
MOTHER: Well? Can you guess it? Turns out he's the one who was barren to begin with. Slow swimmers.
BROTHER/SISTER: No way, I can't believe it ... So sad.
MOTHER [*to* FRANK, *takes his hand*]: So you know, sooner you try the better.
VIA: So did the second wife leave him?

WHAT COMES AFTER SORROW | *Ornella Ohayon*

[*Awkward silence*]
BROTHER [*shocked*]: What?
MOTHER: Why would you say something so awful? [*To* DAD] Wasn't that an awful thing to say darling?
DAD: Awful.
VIA: What? Wait, how – [*to audience*] not worth it, not worth it, not worth it. [*Beat*] How is asking this awful?
MOTHER: Well, why would you wish that on that poor man?
VIA: *He left* his first wife because he thought she was barren.
SISTER: No but she wasn't actually barren. Didn't you listen to the story?
[VIA *glances at the audience*]
FRANK [*genuinely*]: This wine is fantastic.
MOTHER: Ooh well thank you, Frank.
FRANK [*to* VIA *who is hogging the bottle*]: I'd love some more actually if there's still some left –
VIA [*pouring the last of it in her glass*]: Ooh sorry we're actually out.
[EX-BOYFRIEND *enters*]
EX-BOYFRIEND: Sorry, sorry I'm late.
MOTHER: Ooh lovely!
BROTHER: My man! [*Both dudes high five*]
VIA [*to audience*]: Dumped him eight months ago.
[EX-BOYFRIEND *gives* VIA *a quick kiss on the mouth*]
VIA [*to audience*]: He didn't take it very well.
[EX-BOYFRIEND *grabs a chair and sits*]
EX-BOYFRIEND: Traffic was crazy.
VIA [*to* EX-BOYFRIEND]: Hi, hey yeah, hello. Why are you here?
EX-BOYFRIEND: Your mother invited me.
VIA: What? [*To* MOTHER] Mom –
MOTHER: Well, we thought you two could put aside your differences. [*Whispers but not really*] Honey you don't want to show up to your sister's wedding without a date do you?
VIA [*bit less calm*]: Mom, no. You can't just – [*takes a breath, to* EX-BOYFRIEND] I don't want you here.
MOTHER: Now honey you can't turn down people like that. Everyone here at this table is just trying to –
VIA: If you say "help you" one more time I swear to God Mom –

BROTHER: Don't talk to Mom like that!

SISTER: What's wrong with you?

[Beat]

VIA: What's wrong with me is that. [To DAD] Dad, I need my bat mitzvah money. I made a bad call and I can't get myself out of it on my own. And I didn't ask you this before tonight because well I simply lack courage. [To FRANK] And Frank, I'm very sorry, but you're gonna have to postpone the wedding because, I'm just in such a fragile emotional state right now that I can't handle attending my sister's second wedding when I don't even have a date.

[They all stare at each other]

[Beat]

SISTER [to FRANK]: Well, if that's what she needs I mean.

BROTHER: [to DAD] Whatever will help her, right?

[The next few lines VIA says it more to herself than to anyone else]

VIA: Because I don't have a date. And I'm fine. I'm fine and I'm sorry if you're not fine with me being fine just because you wouldn't be fine if *you* were in my shoes. But my shoes ... they're lovely. They're not Gucci but they're lovely. And sometimes, all you can do for someone *if you really want to help them* is to just tell them that you love their shoes. Because their shoes look good on them.

[Beat]

FRANK [to SISTER]: What are we talking about?

SISTER: She's just being dramatic, it'll pass.

BROTHER: Look if you need money for new shoes I'm sure Dad is fine with it, in fact, why don't we all go to the bank next week –

VIA: I won't be in town next week. I am going to New York.

BROTHER: New York?

SISTER: Job interview?

MOTHER: Well that's nice.

VIA: More of a contract signing actually. With a publishing company. That wants to publish my play.

BROTHER: In New York?

VIA: Yes.

BROTHER: Like the city?

VIA: Yes.

SISTER: Wait. Was that your news?
VIA: Yes.
MOTHER: What news?
BROTHER: A publishing company wants to publish your play in New York City.
VIA: That is the news.
SISTER: Like, to the public?
VIA: Yes.
MOTHER: To be read by people.
VIA: Yes.
[Beat]
[They all stare at each other]
MOTHER: Well, what were you waiting for to tell us?

Act 2

[VIA hums Sinatra: "New York, New York"]
VIA [singing]: I'm leaving today ... [She dances a little. A quick pirouette] The guy who wants to publish my play asked me what inspired it and I said everything and nothing at all and he said that he wants me to keep writing from wherever that place was because it's where my humor and my wisdom come from. That made me the happiest I have ever felt in my entire life until he said that still, I have to be *careful*. And I was scared to ask why but I asked why anyways. [Beat] And he said if I lock myself in my art and in my sadness then I might really miss out. And that I didn't have to succeed but that at least I had to *try* to let people love me. But when I look at people I see people like them and I love them but also I love me and it feels like sometimes loving people and loving me are two things that can't go together. [Beat] And when they say things like:
[Everyone comes back on stage for the next line only, then leaves]
EVERYONE: With this brain of yours you could have done something with yourself!
VIA: I just want to scream that I'd give it all up, this brain of mine, and the humor and the wisdom and even my play getting published if it meant I could stop feeling – for one fucking minute

Ornella Ohayon | WHAT COMES AFTER SORROW

– like if joy decided to show up tomorrow I'd be too much of a coward to just ... grab it.
[VIA *breaks*]
VIA: So, I told him what if I let people love me and then I actually like it, and I get so happy that after that nothing I ever write is any good and he doesn't want to publish my plays anymore. [*Beat*] And he didn't say anything for what felt like forever and then he just laughed and he said: "with this brain of yours I doubt it."

THE END

Ce qui vient après le chagrin

VIA: Donc due aux récents évènements j'ai du rendre mon apart et revenir habiter chez ma mère. Depuis ça se passe vraiment ... super. [*Pause*] Une femme super d'ailleurs ma mère. Souvent, elle me dit des trucs du genre:
MOTHER: T'es belle quand tu mets des belles fringues.
VIA: Et comme elle croit bien faire je peux pas vraiment m'énerver et lui répondre que ce qu'elle dit vraiment c'est que sans de belles fringes je suit plutôt moche. Et de toute façon je suis sure que mon ex serait pas d'accord parce qu'il me trouvait toujours particulièrement intéressante quand j'avais pas de fringues du tout. [*Pause*] Bref. [*Pause*]
Depuis, j'essaye vraiment de reprendre ma vie en main. Je passe des entretiens pour des jobs qui servent à rien pour pouvoir me payer un apart qui servirait à beaucoup.
[DAD *éternue*]
VIA: Y a mon père aussi dans la maison. Avec ma mère. Ils font chambre à part et du coup mon père dort dans la plus petite chambre de la maison. Pas juste dans une chambre plus petite que celle de ma mère, mais dans la plus petite des chambres. Dans une maison pleine de chambres. Du coup je dis des trucs du genre je suis revenue habiter chez ma mère alors qu'en vrai je suis revenue chez mes deux parents. [*Pause*] Un gars un peu mélancolique mon daron. Souvent, il me dit des trucs du genre:

WHAT COMES AFTER SORROW | *Ornella Ohayon*

DAD: Avec le cerveau que t'as t'aurais pu faire quelque chose de ta vie.

VIA: En soit c'est plutôt sympa, si vous connaissez mon daron. [*En chuchotant*] Vous ratez rien.

Il dit pas ça méchamment. Il essaye de me dire que je suis intelligente. Il se rend pas compte que ça veut aussi dire que j'ai rien fait de ma vie, sinon il verrait que, ironiquement, ça discrédite ce qu'il dit. Parce que quelqu'un qui foirerait sa vie malgré sa grande intelligence en soit, c'est quelqu'un qui serait vraiment con.

[*L'EX entre en scène. Il marche jusqu'à VIA*]

VIA: Mon ex était con. Mais le genre de con intelligent. Tellement utile d'être comme ça. C'est le genre de personne qui peut supporter d'aller tout le temps à des soirées *et* de taper la discute à tout le monde.

[*L'EX imite un réalisateur de film avec sa caméra*]

Il s'est auto-proclamé producteur de film, le genre de job qui te permet de parler aux gens que tu connais pas et souvent, de dire des trucs du genre:

L'EX: Ton script à l'air d'enfer, appelles mon assistante lundi elle nous organisera un dej'.

VIA: Il a pas d'assistante.

[*L'EX s'en va*]

VIA [*montrant sa robe de soirée*]: Vous vous demandez sûrement pourquoi. Diner de fiançailles de ma sœur ce soir. D'habitude j'essayes d'éviter les réunions familiales de la seule manière possible – en déménageant à l'autre bout du monde – mais hier j'ai reçu une super nouvelle qui pourrait à la fois résoudre tous mes problèmes *et* donner un sens à mon existence. Du coup j'ai décidé d'y aller. [*Pause*] Et puis, c'est le diner de fiançailles de ma sœur. Pour un futur mariage- pansement. Etrange, je sais. Deux mots qui vont pas trop ensemble. Mais ma frangine a le genre d'intelligence qu'on voit grâce à ses très gros diplômes donc le fait qu'elle soit absolument incapable de rester seule plus que trois minutes et demies ... on choisit de pas en parler. [*Pause*] Souvent, elle me dit des trucs du genre:

SISTER: En vrai tu devrais me remercier.

VIA: Et quand je dis "pourquoi" elle a tendance à dire des trucs du genre:
SISTER: Au moins avec mon divorce ils ont arrêté de te faire chier.
VIA: Elle a divorcé il y a trois mois. On s'est dit qu'ils devaient plus aimer grand chose en commun mais le problème venait en fait du seul truc en commun qu'ils aimaient. Les hommes. [*Pause*]
Ma sœur elle, arrive à être belle même quand elle met pas des belles fringues et quand elle nous a annoncé qu'elle se remarierait alors que son divorce n'était même pas encore prononcé on était tous tellement surpris qu'on s'est surpris à lui organiser une soirée surprise.

To the Zoom and Back

Cindi Sansone-Braff

Cast

AVA LUCELLO: a woman in her early seventies
THOMAS CHATON: a man in his early seventies
OFFSTAGE VOICE OF ROBIN: a woman in her early thirties.

Setting

The play takes place in two separate Long Island locations simultaneously during a Zoom virtual date, one evening in April 2020. At rise: AVA's hair is well-coiffed, and she is neatly yet conservatively dressed. She's fumbling with her cell phone setting up for her Zoom virtual date. It's obvious she has never Zoomed before. THOMAS is still handsome, albeit balding, and dressed in a suit and tie. He's sitting calmly in front of his computer, ready to Zoom. The audience and THOMAS see some pretty unattractive angles of AVA's face; for instance: the camera is under her chin, then up her nose, and then her video image turns upside down.

AVA: Robin! Now the video's upside down.
ROBIN [*off*]: Auntie Ava, just do what I showed you before. Turn the portrait orientation lock off. [*Ava fumbles, then uprights the video. She puts on her mask and starts gloving up*] It's a virtual date. You don't need PPE.
AVA: Oh … Oh … OK. I'm just worried I could be a super-spreader. [*Music cue: The second movement of Beethoven's Seventh Symphony begins playing*] Oh … Oh … I … I didn't know you was already here. Hi there, Mr. Chaton … um … Tom. [*Seeing herself in the video, she begins futzing with her hair*]
THOMAS: Thomas. I prefer Thomas.
AVA: Well, Thomas, it's 6.45pm on the dot. You're very prompt. That's a good trait, right? My sister, Concetta, *riposi in pace*, always claimed it was. All my life, she hounded me about my

tardiness. "Ava, when you're not dilly-dallying, you're lollygagging!" Speaking of my dearly departed big sister, that music you're playing, makes me feel like I'm in Maloney's funeral parlor viewing an open casket.

THOMAS: It's *Allegretto* from Beethoven's Seventh. Richard Wagner felt this symphony was "the apotheosis of dance."

AVA: Well ... Ava Lucello thinks it sounds like something the priest is gonna play while he's giving me Last Rites.

THOMAS: I thought we could use a little mood music.

AVA: If you're in the mood for the morgue, then that burial hymn hits a home run. To set the right tone for a first date – not so much.

THOMAS [*music cue: Thomas shuts off the music*]: Your dating profile said that you love listening to good music.

AVA: Oh, my ... my niece, Robin, wrote that up. I'm not too good with computers. Yes ... yes, she's right though. I like good music. I like *The Voice*.

THOMAS: The what?

AVA: *The Voice*. A reality TV show, you know, a singing competition. It's got Blake Shelton on it. I really like him. [*There's an awkward pause*] You seem very relaxed. I guess you've done this kind of thing before.

THOMAS: Virtual dating? I don't think anyone in the history of humankind has done this kind of thing before. My son, the self-anointed matchmaker, signed me up on the Forever Young Dating Site. He says, "To find love in the time of Corona, you've got to think outside the lockdown."

AVA: So, what made *you* tap the match button on *me*?

THOMAS: You have the same first name as my wife.

AVA: You're still married? Your profile said you was widowed! I don't remember you mentioning nothing about your wife making a miraculous resurrection from the grave.

THOMAS: Oh, no! She didn't do that. Ava's still dead. I mean, she died ... my wife ... five years ago ... breast cancer.

AVA: Please accept my sincerest condolences to you and your family.

THOMAS: Thank you. And how about you? What made you want to match up with me?

TO THE ZOOM AND BACK | *Cindi Sansone-Braff*

AVA: I thought you had ... in your picture ... very kind eyes.
THOMAS: Your profile says you're into cooking.
AVA: I don't know if I'm *into* cooking. I cook. You know, the basic stuff ... meat and potatoes ... pasta and sauce. Your profile said ... you enjoy gourmet dining and travel.
THOMAS: Yes, Ava and I, my Ava, we traveled around the world dining in some of the finest restaurants ... Osteria Francescana in Italy, the Arzak in Spain, and even Le Chateaubriand in France. According to your profile, you like to travel as well.
AVA: Oh, I do. Last year, me and Robin took the Greyhound to Atlantic City. We stayed three days and two nights at the Tropicana. And the year before that, we spent a few days at Disney World.
THOMAS: Your profile also mentioned that you enjoy the theatre. I was over the moon to have secured tickets to *The Cherry Orchard*, at New York City Center, but it canceled. You know, COVID-19 strikes again.
AVA: In March, right before the whole world slammed shut, me and my niece drove over to Miller Place High School to see *Mamma Mia!* The whole audience was singing along with the kids. It was great! [*Singing*] "So when you're near me, darling, can't you hear me, S.O.S."
THOMAS [*a long pause*]: Your profile said you were single.
AVA: It sounded better than spinster. That's what my sister always called me, but I kept telling her, "That's not a politically correct thing to say no more," but on her deathbed, the last thing she said to me was, "*Addio*, spinster."
THOMAS: Do you have any children?
AVA: I just toldcha, I was never married.
THOMAS: That doesn't mean you couldn't have children.
AVA: Oh, in my world, it does. I was raised in a very strict, Italian, Catholic household. You know, first comes love, then comes marriage, then comes Ava with a baby carriage.
THOMAS: But I take it that you're close with your niece, Robin.
AVA: That goes without saying. She's like my own daughter. She lives upstairs, in my mother's old apartment. She's a good girl.
THOMAS: How old is she?

AVA: Thirty-three. Her birthday was yesterday. Robin's single, but that's not seen as a bad thing no more. I felt bad for her being stuck in a foxhole with me on her birthday. So, I called up Uber Eats and got takeout from Applebee's, and the two of us made the best of it. It's been really hard for her ... her shop isn't deemed an essential service, so she can't even make a living right now.

THOMAS: What does she do?

AVA: Hair. She's a beautician. She's a very good one. Let me tell you. I'm lucky to be in lockdown with her. My friends are all complaining about the sorry state of their hair right now.

THOMAS: I guess being bald has its upside.

AVA: Robin insists upon doing my hair, every week, just like always.

THOMAS: Your hair looks very nice.

AVA: Thank you. I'll tell her. Well, this has been –

THOMAS: – the new normal.

AVA: Tom ... I mean Thomas. Take a look-see! Over there! By your bay window! There's a Cardinal. As kids, we was always told ... when you spot a Cardinal, it's a sign from your loved ones on the Other Side.

THOMAS: I don't really believe in any of that psychic hocus-pocus, but my grandson does. Every time he sees a Cardinal, he shouts, "It's Grandma Ava coming by to say, 'Hi!' "

AVA: I guess ... sometimes it's kinda nice to think that ... maybe ... they're still around. Well, I know I'm not what you expected. I'm boring. There's not much to me. What you see is what you get. Whereas you ... now you've been around the world! You listen to Beethoven, not because you have to, but because you want to. You've dined like a king, had a wife, and a family. The most exciting thing that ever happened to me was back in 1984 when I won 500 dollars in a scratch-off. I just wantcha to know ... this has been fun for me, but like I says, I'm boring.

THOMAS: That is the one word I wouldn't use to describe you. We're two consenting adults, right? And we're both in agreement that this has been ... fun. Then, maybe, we should shoot for a second date?

AVA: Really?

THOMAS: Your profile said you're from South Huntington. I don't live too far from you ... Lloyd Harbor. Tomorrow, I could be the designated drive-by-food guy and swing by your house at 6.15pm sharp to drop off dinner. We'll say a quick in-person hello, all masked and gloved up, and just in case you're a super-spreader, to be doubly safe, we'll social distance.

AVA: Like I always say, "Better six feet apart than six feet under."

THOMAS: After I drop off your food, I'll head home and join you for a virtual dinner. I just need your address.

AVA: Oh. I don't know about that. I barely know you.

ROBIN [*off*]: Auntie Ava ... the man is *bringing* you food. He's not Hannibal the Cannibal. Tell him you'll message him your address later.

AVA: Sorry about the interruption. Robin insisted on chaperoning. It seems her best friend, Ashley, had a virtual date that didn't turn out so hot.

ROBIN [*off*]: The guy was sitting there with no pants on with the camera angled down.

AVA: I told her, "It should only happen to me!"

THOMAS: You should have put that in your profile, "Clothes optional." You would have gotten a lot of likes. Now, Ms. Lucello, what kind of food would you like me to bring?

AVA: Oh, me. I'm not fussy. Growing up, we had two choices in the Lucello's La cucina: "Take it or leave it and like it or lump it. My pops was famous throughout Staten Island for screaming ... on the top of his lungs ... every suppertime like clockwork. [*Imitating a heavy Italian accent*] "Johnny-Boy, y'wanna be eating or y'wanna beating?" Being Johnny-Boy's little sister and watching him take all them whippings, I was so scared sitting at the supper table, I swear, if my mother served shit on a shingle, I would've swallowed it! So, if y'treating, I'm eating!

THOMAS: I'll bring plenty for Robin, too.

ROBIN [*off*]: Thank you, Thomas. Just remember, I don't eat mushrooms or anything with eyes.

THOMAS: It's a date then! Tomorrow evening, at 6.45pm on the dot, we'll dine ... separately but together.

AVA: Is this gonna be another Ten-Minute-Zoom-Speed-Date? Because if I shovel food down that fast, I'm gonna wind up with a wicked case of agita.

THOMAS: No, it's going to be a real virtual date. Light some candles, break open a bottle of wine, and pick a playlist from *The Voice*.

AVA: In that case, I'll break out my mother's good china and her mother's good silver. What am I saving them for?

ROBIN [*off*]: Me! I thought you said you were saving them for *me*!

THOMAS: I'll put on my white tie and tails, and I don't want our dinner getting cold, so whatever you do, Ava, try not to lollygag.

AVA: OK, Thomas, but don't hold it against me if I dilly-dally. It's my nature. *Ciao* for now, Bello!

THOMAS: Au revoir, Mademoiselle!

THE END

Más allá del Zoom

Personajes

AVA LUCELLO: Una mujer con poco más de setenta años
TOMÁS CHATON: Un hombre con poco más de setenta años
VOZ DE ROBIN: Una mujer con poco más de treinta años.

Escenario

Esta obra se lleva a cabo simultáneamente en dos lugares de Long Island, NY durante una cita virtual por Zoom. Abril 2020, por la tarde. Se abre el telón: Ava está bien arreglada y peinada, vestida de una manera conservadora. Se encuentra en una batalla por descifrar cómo utilizar Zoom desde su celular, para poder conectarse a su cita virtual. Es obvio que es su primera vez usando esta aplicación. TOMÁS, a pesar de su calvicie, es buen mozo. Está vestido con un terno y una corbata. Está calmado y sentado al frente de su computadora, listo para empezar su cita. La audiencia y TOMÁS ven ciertos ángulos poco atractivos de la cara de AVA, por ejemplo: la cámara enfoca su quijada, su nariz y luego la imagen de su video está al revés.

AVA: ¡Robin! El video está al revés.
ROBIN [*voz en off*]: Tía Ava, solo haz lo que te enseñé anteriormente. Ponlo en modo vertical y bloquéalo. [*AVA batalla con su celular, y logra poner la cámara de manera vertical. Se pone su mascarilla e incluso unos guantes*] Es una cita virtual. No necesitas usar protección para el virus.
AVA: Oh ... Oh ... OK. Solo me preocupa ser propagadora del virus. [*Señal musical: El segundo movimiento de la séptima sinfonía de Beethoven empieza a sonar*] Oh ... Oh ... yo ...yo no sabía que ya estabas conectado. Hola, Mr. Chaton ... um ... Tom. [*Ava se ve en la cámara, ella empieza a jugar con su cabello*]
TOMÁS: Tomás. Prefiero que me digan Tomás.
AVA: Bueno, Tomás, son exactamente las 6.45 de la tarde, ¡Eres puntual! ¿Es una buena cualidad, cierto? Mi hermana, Concetta, *riposi in pace*, siempre dijo que lo era. Toda mi vida, ella me repetía siempre que yo era muy impuntual y que llegaba tarde a todos lados. "Ava, siempre estás en las nubes". Hablando de mi querida y difunta hermana mayor, la música que está sonando me hace sentir que estoy en una funeraria de Maloney viendo la tapa abierta de un féretro.
TOMÁS: Es Allegretto de la séptima sinfonía de Beethoven. Richard Wagner considera que esta sinfonía es majestuosa.
AVA: Bueno ... Ava Lucello piensa que esta melodía es algo que el sacerdote entona mientras está haciendo los ritos funerarios.
TOMÁS: Yo pensé que nosotros podíamos escuchar un poco de música relajada y romántica y por eso la puse.
AVA: Quizás si estuviéramos en la morgue, entonces el himno burial sería perfecto o ideal. Pero para ponerlo de entrada para una primera cita ... no lo creo.
TOMÁS [*señal musical: TOMÁS apaga la música*]: Tu perfil de citas decía que te gustaba escuchar buena música
AVA: Oh, mi sobrina, Robin, escribió eso. Yo no soy muy buena con la computadora. Pero, sí, ella tiene razón, me gusta la buena música, como la de *La Voz*.

TOMÁS: ¿La qué?

AVA: *La Voz,* un reality de televisión, tú sabes, una competencia de canto. Blake Shelton participó ahí, él realmente me gusta. [*Silencio incómodo entre los dos*] Te noto relajado, asumo que ya has tenido citas virtuales antes.

TOMÁS: ¿Citas virtuales? No creo que nadie en la historia de la humanidad haya hecho algo como esto antes. Mi hijo, que se describe como un cupido del siglo XXI, me suscribió a la página citas *Siempre Joven*. Él dice, "Para encontrar amor en tiempos de Corona, debes pensar fuera del encierro."

AVA: Entonces ... ¿Qué fue lo que te gustó de mí?

TOMÁS: Tu primer nombre es igual al de mi esposa.

AVA: ¿Cómo? ¿Aún estás casado? ¡Tu perfil decía que estabas viudo! No recuerdo que hayas mencionado nada acerca de una milagrosa resurrección de tu esposa.

TOMÁS: ¡Oh no! No es eso, Ava aún continúa muerta, ella murió hace cinco años atrás de cáncer de seno.

AVA: Por favor, acepta mis más sinceras condolencias para ti y tu familia.

(Translated by Natasha Astudillo)

The People's Toast: A Contemporization of Václav Havel's Vaněk Plays

Ellis Stump

Cast

FRAN VANĚKA: twenties to thirties, female, writer, activist, traveler
ALEK: sixties, male, restaurant manager and "coffeemaster"
VERA: around the same age as VANĚKA, female, social media influencer
MICHAL: around the same age as VERA, male, tech startup coder
PHONE: AI voice, like Siri.

Setting

An outdoor sidewalk bistro in Prague, Czech Republic. Present time.

1. The People's Toast

[*At a bistro along the sidewalk, umbrellas stretch over tables topped with plastic menus. The atmosphere is not fancy, swank, or contemporary, but rather, slightly shabby yet sincere. The restaurant manager* ALEK *is writing upon an A-frame sign, advertising the daily special: Avocado toast.* VANĚKA *enters with a to-go coffee, smoking a cigarette, passing the entrance. Then, an automated voice from her phone – like Siri – speaks up*]
PHONE: Stop walking. You have arrived at your destination. [*Surprised,* VANĚKA *falters abruptly. She paces onward a few steps to finish and dispose of her cigarette, while her phone continues reprimanding*] Stop walking. You have arrived at your –
VANĚKA: Shhh! I know!
ALEK [*noticing her*]: Vaněka? You're Fran Vaněka?
VANĚKA: Yes, *ahoj*. Hello. Guilty as charged.

ALEK: Can I call ya Fran?
VANĚKA: No, yeah. I don't mind –
ALEK: "No, yeah?" *Ne* or *ano*? That's American slang, isn't that? Every word you all babble over there is so back and forth. Wishy-washy. It's so ... What's the word?
VANĚKA: Um, unintentional, indecisive, ambiguous?
ALEK: Wishy-washy. That's the one I was looking for.
VANĚKA: Oh. Yeah. That would suffice.
ALEK [*with a scoff*]: Suffice.
VANĚKA: I'm sorry? Did I –
ALEK: I'm Aleksander, the manager. The boss. As if anyone cares. Here, little lady. Have a seat. Have a drink. Let's toast. Cheers to your new home. [*ALEK leads her to a table, pours two glasses, and downs his immediately*]
VANĚKA: Thank you. It's lovely. [*Opposite him, she sips gingerly*]
ALEK: Ha. Now don't mock me like that. Don't ... What's the word I'm looking for?
VANĚKA: Condescend? Patronize? Satire?
ALEK: No, just ... Just don't mock me like that. I know this isn't the trendy coffee shop scene you're used to. The Café Starbucks, where you worked last. Saw that on your resume.
VANĚKA: Oh, I actually quite dislike corporate chains. I applied here intentionally, to support a traditional, local, family-centric spot. I only worked at Starbucks till I could find another job.
ALEK: But of course. You can afford those places, so you don't like 'em.
VANĚKA: That's not quite it, actually –
ALEK: Hey now, I don't need to know your personal history. Don't know it. Don't need to.
VANĚKA: Thank you. I appreciate that.
ALEK: But I do know you're a felon. Saw that on your resume.
VANĚKA: That wasn't on my –
ALEK: In the application, little lady. Now why'd you write that?
VANĚKA: I am legally obligated to.
ALEK: I mean, why'd you write all that *hloupost* that got you in trouble?
VANĚKA: Oh. Uh, I feel humanly obligated to.

THE PEOPLE'S TOAST | *Ellis Stump*

ALEK: You're a dissident, or whatever they're calling themselves these days. You were one of 'em in the States. An activist.

VANĚKA: I suppose. It's 2020. Everyone's an activist.

ALEK: But you were screaming? Protesting? Got caught?

VANĚKA: Guilty as charged.

ALEK: Against their president, old Donald Trump. For immigration, and climate change, and all that *hloupost*. I see that on the news.

VANĚKA: No, yeah. For claiming to know nothing of my personal history, you seem to actually know quite a lot –

ALEK: Are you gonna do that back here in Prague now? With President Miloš Zeman?

VANĚKA: Oh, I, to be honest –

PHONE: Stop walking. You have arrived at your destination.

VANĚKA: Sorry. I'll silence, um … [*Silencing her phone*] I'm so sorry about that.

ALEK: Don't be sorry, kid, be proud! He's got a mansion for crying out loud! A couple mansions, don't he? All marble and Renaissance gold. And a supermodel wife with platinum hair and designer sunglasses inside each one, like a glossy, polished little doll. A couple, probably.

VANĚKA: I'm sorry, who?

ALEK: President Donald Trump, kid! Come on! Don't you want a couple?

VANĚKA: Supermodel wives? Um, perhaps, if they consented to –

ALEK: No, Fran! Mansions! Don't you want a couple mansions?

VANĚKA: Oh. I wouldn't know what to do with only one mansion.

ALEK [*scoff*]: You wouldn't know what to do with only one mansion.

VANĚKA: I would not.

ALEK: You'd live in it, little lady! *Legrační*. Can you even operate a basic coffee machine?

VANĚKA: No, yeah, I can.

ALEK: And now where'd you learn that?

VANĚKA: Uh, Starbucks. You saw that on my resume, didn't you?

ALEK [*scoff*]: Your resume.

VANĚKA: I'm sorry, was it weak? I can forward you my updated CV in PDF format, linked to my cover letter and multimedia PowerPoint, if you'd like. But if not, no worries –

Ellis Stump | THE PEOPLE'S TOAST

ALEK: Is that what they're teaching you at the universities these days? How to write a cover letter but not operate a basic coffee machine? *Legrační.* [ALEK *begins refilling the glasses, to* VANĚKA's *dismay. She struggled to finish hers*] Here, kid, relax. Have another drink, and I'll tell you a bit of our history. Then I'll teach ya how to fold utensils into a napkin and toss a side salad in a flash and change the daily specials board. You smoke?

VANĚKA [*relieved, reaching for her cigarettes*]: I thought, of all these questions, you'd never ask. I only do while walking but –

ALEK: You shouldn't.

VANĚKA: Smoke? Or walk? Or ask questions?

ALEK: Now you're talkin'. Let's toast. Cheers to the establishment! [*After gulping*] We've been here a hundred years, kid. We're part of Prague. This is where, back in the day, folks would come to toast their sloshy pitchers and play cards and catch up on the latest films and sports, not just type away alone on their computer keyboards. To ask each other about their families and wives, not Twitter about politics. To get along, not dissent. Here we're a family, as you can see. A family *for* the families. But of course, we've had to adapt to modern demand, you see. We have to ... What's the word I'm looking for? It's on the tip of my tongue, so the beer keeps getting in the way. What's the word?

VANĚKA: Entertain? Adhere? Appease?

ALEK: We have to adapt! See here; we've gotta craft "artisan delicacies." We have to make *brunch*. Not breakfast or lunch, but this brand-new invention of yours, brunch. Quinoa bowls. Kale bowls. Millennials, for some reason, want everything in a bowl. And avocado toast. You worship avocado toast. I have to serve goddamned avocado toast!

VANĚKA: Yes, I see that. On the sign.

ALEK: Ignore the sign, Fran.

VANĚKA: Alright.

ALEK: But hey, Fran, we still stay true to our original establishment and values.

VANĚKA: I believe you. It's honestly quite important and impressive, I believe, cooperating past with progress –

PHONE: Stop walking. You have arrived at your destination.

VANĚKA: Sorry. I'm so sorry about that.

THE PEOPLE'S TOAST | *Ellis Stump*

ALEK: Now, I don't give a thick flimsy slice of your Mexican vegetable bread –

VANĚKA: Avocado toast? Avocados are actually a fruit –

ALEK: If you're a felon, Fran.

VANĚKA: I appreciate that ...

ALEK: I don't need to know your personal history; keep that to yourself. But I do know you write. Saw that on your resume, and the Internet. You don't believe I can read FaceSpace and Twitter and all that *hloupost* but I do. Some of your little stories have been in the *New York Times*.

VANĚKA: Yes.

ALEK: And plays in the big city theaters.

VANĚKA: Off-off-off-Broadway, but sure. It's 2020. Everyone's an intellectual. Everyone's had a story in the *New York Times*. My few that have been picked up, mean nothing, pay nothing –

ALEK: Everyone, you say? Millennials, Fran. Not me, kid. Here, have another drink, and tell me what you mean by that, everyone's an intellectual?

VANĚKA: Oh. Well ... Any of us who could mash even three words together back in grade school, the quiet kids, who kept to the corners in kindergarten, crafting or reading, we were dubbed "Gifted" by the system and praised by our parents, who worked steadily all those years so we could take risks, who encouraged us to jet overseas and earn MFAs in Creative Writing which I'm still not sure differs from any other kind of writing, and there, we learned how to write objectively subjective theses, not personal statements or cover letters.

ALEK: You think that's bad, Fran?

VANĚKA: No. Just ... uniquely challenging.

ALEK: We've been here a hundred years, little lady. We're part of Prague, and history, but you don't believe me.

VANĚKA: Yeah, no, I do.

ALEK: Can you even operate a basic coffee machine?

VANĚKA: No, yeah. I can.

ALEK: I'll teach you how to fold utensils into a napkin, and toss a side salad in a flash, and change the daily specials board.

VANĚKA: Alright.

ALEK: Back in the day, it used to be the Boss says "Run" and the employees ask "How far?" Now, the Boss says anything, and you Millennials just blink back blankly with your bowls for eyes and babble: "Why?"

VANĚKA: I'm sorry.

ALEK: And that! You all say sorry too much. *Legracani*.

VANĚKA: Oh uh, yeah, sorry. I'm sorry. We're sorry. Ah! Sorry.

ALEK: Damn, it's so ... The beer has numbed the taste buds at the tip of tongue. What's the word?

VANĚKA: Self-deprecating? Cynical? Uniquely depressing?

ALEK: No, come on, spit it out, it's so ...

VANĚKA: Oh, maybe you mean: Ironic? Contrasting? Collateral?

ALEK: No. It's ... Sad. Sad. You're intellectuals, right, little lady? You know your value. You know you're safe. So why feel bad?

VANĚKA: Because that value is worthless in the current economy.

ALEK: And what *isn't*, Fran, ya intellectual?

VANĚKA: Uh ... Avocado toast?

ALEK: We have to adapt! We have to make *bowls* and bow down to *brunch*. I know this isn't your regular trendy scene. Your fancy-shmancy Salon Starbucks in the Sky.

VANĚKA: Oh, I actually quite dislike corporate chains. I applied here, to support a traditional, local, family-centric spot. I only worked at Starbucks /until I could find another job – /

ALEK: / Until you could steal another / ... Smoke?

VANĚKA: I thought, of all these questions, you'd never –

[*Sighing, VANĚKA shakes out a cigarette. But ALEK swipes it from her fingers and flings it across the stage*]

ALEK: Don't you want a couple, Fran? [ALEK *now either lights up himself or takes a long drink, ignoring* VANĚKA'*s following questions.*]

VANĚKA: A couple what? Jobs, we were musing upon? Well, in this empty gig wasteland, sure. Everyone I know juggles two, three or four if they're lucky –

ALEK: No, Fran, a couple *mansions*! You treasure your dirty little flats, you Millennials, and to live out of rented cars. You don't want a house. You can afford those places, so you don't like 'em.

VANĚKA: Actually, I'd love a house. Space. But I don't *need* it, and can't possibly afford it –

THE PEOPLE'S TOAST | *Ellis Stump*

ALEK: Where do you live anyway?
VANĚKA: I live in a hostel. A few stops away.
ALEK: American tourist.
VANĚKA: Actually, I'm a returning local.
ALEK: I don't know that. Don't need to. All I need to know is you fled your mother country like you leave your mother parents, just one in your *zeitgeist* of stubborn smart kids.
VANĚKA: Resilient. Optimistic, ambitious humans –
ALEK: Because you can afford to be. I can't.
VANĚKA*:* And about that, I'm sorry.
ALEK: You say sorry too much. You all do, as you keep moving and crashing place to place and all that *hloupost*. Meanwhile, I've sat here a hundred years, little lady. [*On "sat," ALEK may stand and pace, sloppily bumping into things*] Didn't have no teachers calling me smart. No participation trophies, or even ribbons or participation high-fives. My folks couldn't ship me off to the States for an MFA IPA whatever. I got to work here and considered myself lucky, you know? At a cushy café instead of in a factory, operating a basic coffee machine instead of a massive conveyor belt. Tossing salads instead of constructing buildings. Changing this here sidewalk sign with daily specials instead of the train station board with daily delays. Nobody cares or praises or encourages me to take risks. I've been here a hundred years, little lady. Your texts and Twitters don't last longer than a minute.
VANĚKA [*quietly, aside*]: I actually quite dislike social media.
ALEK: I am the manager, the boss, but now the boss says "Run" and the employees and the automated cash registers stare back and demand "Why?" Donald Trump, Fran, and President Miloš Zeman – they're the People's Politicians. They don't blink. And yet, here you are, planning to do that back in Prague now with your mother country's current father Miloš Zeman. Write your big stories and plays.
VANĚKA: Perhaps I should be leaving ...
ALEK [*while pouring out the pitcher upon the table*]: No! You can't! You have to have one more drink! Cheers to your ... Cheers to *our* ...
VANĚKA: Thank you. But actually, I'd prefer ...

ALEK: What, Fran? A kale smoothie? A crafty little beer? An IPA MFA?

VANĚKA: I suppose just another coffee to-go, if anything?

ALEK: A coffee. *Legračni* ... [*After a long beat*] I don't know how to operate the basic coffee machine. [*Another long beat*] So, what exactly *are* you doing here, you protesting, screaming, fighting, mocking, adapting, wishy-washy, sad, *legračni,* New York Times writing intellectual?

VANĚKA: Uh, well. Since I quite dislike social media, I'm pretty much barred from any corporate career. Not like I'd know what to do with a mansion, or even want to know. I just need enough sustenance to survive, in order to help others thrive –

PHONE: Stop walking ...

VANĚKA: To write words for the people, that will improve and progress our situations. But I'm no martyr; it's for me, too. Despite everything, despite my economic worthlessness in this gig wasteland, I still feel, deep down, those words hold meaning.

PHONE: *Stop talking* ...

VANĚKA: I still feel excited, inspired, and driven to wake up each day and hit the ground running, put pen to new paper, or raw fingers to worn-down keys, mashing letters into messages. And I still, god forbid guilty as charged, feel humanly obligated to share them. I still –

PHONE: *Stop talking, Vaněka! you have arrived at your* –

VANĚKA: Sorry. I'm sorry about that. I'm ... [*Suddenly embracing chippier, can-do enthusiasm*] overflowing with enthusiasm to begin work, Alek! Manager! Boss! This place has been here a hundred years! Can ya teach me how to change the daily specials board?!

ALEK [*matching her energy, gleeful*]: Why of course, little lady! [*Cheerful beat, before he drops drastically back to his usual glum self*] It's avocado toast every day.

[*Moment of silence.* ALEK *finishes his beer.* VANĚKA *frowns. Lights fade*]

PHONE: You have arrived at your destination.

THE PEOPLE'S TOAST | *Ellis Stump*

2. Shavasana

[*VANĚKA, wearing an apron, folds utensils in napkins at the table. She appears comfortable, even relaxed, though slightly bored. She's worked there a while. After a moment, a hip Gen Z couple – VERA and MICHAL – enter boisterously and flamboyantly. When they see VANĚKA, they squeal with happiness. Startled, VANĚKA fumbles and sends forks flying*]

VERA: Vaněka! Honey! Hi!

VANĚKA: Wow, uh, hello! Vera, Michal, what're you doing here – ?

VERA: We saw you work here now. Your mom announced it on Facebook.

VANĚKA: Oh. Yikes.

MICHAL: We thought you were still stuck in the slammer, man. We hate to have you serve us.

VERA: You can just fetch us what we want, and bring it over when it's ready.

VANĚKA: That's um, pretty much my job –

MICHAL: But no rush, man, no pressure.

VERA: And if you want anything, go ahead and order on us, honey.

VANĚKA: Oh, I couldn't –

MICHAL: Fran!

VERA: Treat yourself! You look like you could use a plain black coffee. [*To MICHAL*] Babe, check it out! They serve avocado toast! And breakfast bowls!

MICHAL: Fran, you should see how Vera combines those two artisan delicacies into one. She bakes the toast, carefully spreads the avocado slices on top, and then mashes all that together with a mortar and pestle set and plates the grounds in a pretty bowl over quinoa and kale.

VERA: Do they do that here?

VANĚKA: Oh, I don't believe so –

VERA: They should! Ask "why not?" instead of "what if?" and try that nourishing dish.

MICHAL: Preach, man. It's so simple.

VERA: So pure. You can whip it up in a flash!

MICHAL: Vera meal-preps bento boxes she takes to hot yoga.

VERA [*modeling her getup, extending a leg upon the table*]: What do you think, honey, of my ensemble?

VANĚKA: It's um, very nice.

VERA: Have you tried it yet? Hot yoga? You haven't, *obviously* –

VANĚKA: Yeah no, I have not.

VERA: Oh my god, you absolutely, totally must! It cleanses and detoxifies our lives and souls, Fran. Believe us. It keeps us simple and grounded.

MICHAL: It takes this difficult challenge and makes it even *harder*. We're obsessed with that.

VERA: As for how hard – I can see you begging the question, honey – well, you'd just have to observe Michal in his leggings ...

[*VERA wiggles her brows. MICHAL giggles. VANĚKA stands by, uncomfortable*]

MICHAL: Seriously, Fran man, how fresh and wet do you feel, after overcoming a session like that?

VERA: The literal steaminess translates seamlessly into our sex situation. We think you may appreciate that stimulation and purification. We care about your health, honey.

MICHAL: We care about downward-facing dog.

[*MICHAL wiggles his brows. VERA giggles. VANĚKA fidgets, uncomfortably*]

VANĚKA: So, uh, can I get you two anything, or ... ?

MICHAL: We hate to have you serve us. You can just fetch us – well, I guess we'll start with drinks – two mimosas.

VANĚKA: Alright.

VERA: And two for me, as well.

MICHAL: And I'll take a cappuccino.

VERA: And I'll just start with a vanilla caramel mocha latte with soy milk and chocolate swirls and extra foam on top. Skim. Just bring them over when they're ready.

VANĚKA [*scrambling to take order*] That's ... yeah, pretty much ... my job –

MICHAL: But no rush, man. No pressure.

VANĚKA: We care about your health. We're obsessed with ...

MICHAL [*to VERA, as if it's an inside joke*]: Downward-facing dog ...

THE PEOPLE'S TOAST | *Ellis Stump*

[*Chuckling,* MICHAL *and* VERA *gaze into each other's eyes, endeared.* VANĚKA *backs away awkwardly, disappearing into the restaurant. Immediately upon her exit,* MICHAL *and* VERA's *giddiness dissipates into absolutely nothing, a flat emotionless void, as they stare blankly at their phones. Only once* VANĚKA *returns do they come alive again*]

VERA: Oh my god, Michal babe, behold these beverages! We better toast at once.

VANĚKA: To what?

VERA: You can use my water, honey.

[VERA *hands* VANĚKA *her water, while she and* MICHAL *struggle to juggle their various fancy-shmancy beverages. They snap some pictures in various poses. No toast occurs. Then, out of nowhere,* VERA *brightly regards* VANĚKA]

VERA: So, why *are* you working here now, honey?

VANĚKA: Uh, for money, I guess. Groceries. Rent – my mom's. I live with her now. Cigarettes.

MICHAL: Fran!

VERA: Cigarettes are absolutely totally terrible for you!

MICHAL: It's 2020. Nobody smokes cigarettes. [MICHAL *hits off on a Juul or dab pen*]

VERA: We care about your health, honey.

MICHAL: We're obsessed with downward-facing dog.

VERA: And rent? Prague costs nothing for millennials, Fran. A flat is so cheap, they're basically handing them out.

VANĚKA: If you pay for one …

VERA: They fling fresh fruit from the sidewalks!

VANĚKA: If you pay for it … And by "they," you mean – ?

VERA: You've watched our renovations on my Instagram story, right? I'm an influencer now, obviously. People love seeing others self-love. So, I offer tours of our bright airy space packed with all our house plants and minimalist decor. We have massive amounts of minimalist decor. Maximum minimalism, mama. Have you come by, virtually?

VANĚKA: I have not.

MICHAL: Fran! That's offensive.

Ellis Stump | THE PEOPLE'S TOAST

VERA: It is! You absolutely, totally must. Michal just jetted over to Amsterdam last weekend for this hot and trendy music festival. EDM, right, babe?

MICHAL: The music's so loud, you don't even have to acknowledge each other. It's lit. [*Hitting his Juul*]

VERA: He bought a bunch of vintage records we hung up on one of our backdrop walls, Fran. We have a whole collection.

VANĚKA: Oh, I'd actually love to hear those.

MICHAL: Of course, we don't have a record player.

VERA: But we do have a spin bike that insults you every morning, subscription to a smoothie shaker service that ships you the latest model every week, speakers that stream positive mantras directly into your ear canals at random, and a bidet. That's all one machine.

VANĚKA: Sounds like the Ritz-Carlton.

VERA: Vaněka, honey, the Ritz doesn't have bidets.

MICHAL: Everything is voice-automated. You just tell our Siri what to do.

VERA: And it all connects to Michal's watch. Watch!

[MICHAL *holds up his wrist eagerly, but* VANĚKA *begins stepping away*]

VANĚKA: I'm uh, going to slip inside, actually, check on the other tables –

VERA: Oh my god! What? No!

MICHAL: Dude! You can't.

VERA: You absolutely totally can't.

VANĚKA: But the other tables –

VERA: But *our* table, Fran!

MICHAEL: What about us? Capital U.S.??!

VERA: We have ...

MICHAEL: *More to order!*

VERA: We have *more to order*, Fran!

VANĚKA: Alright, alright, alright. So ... Can I get you two anything, or ... ?

MICHAL: Fran. We hate to have you serve us.

VERA: Why are you working here anyway?

MICHAL: Why not just score a gig at a start-up, like me?

Borderless Thalia

THE PEOPLE'S TOAST | *Ellis Stump*

VERA: It's 2020, honey. Everyone works for a dying start-up. If you coded like Michal, you could type all day, like a laborious little robot, just like you love! You'd be obsessed with that.

VANĚKA: That's uh, not really the typing I prefer –

VERA: We know, Fran. You do your sweet little ... [*Trailing off, looking to* MICHAL *for help*]

MICHAL [*genuinely unsure, but trying to help*]: Stories?

VERA: Whatever they're called.

MICHAL [*now back to* VANĚKA]: Dude. Why not just write at the *New York Times*?

VERA: Of course, it's because they only publish and pay their most popular content producers –

VANĚKA: No, yeah. Pretty much.

VERA: Oh my god! You should start a *blog*!

MICHAL: We have a podcast. We sit down together and record weekly.

VERA: It cleanses and detoxifies our lives and souls, Fran.

MICHAL: You should totally write something like that, man. For all your activist ... *hloupost*.

VERA: Put that on the Internet where it belongs!

MICHAL: Finally kick it off the ground! It'll be so simple.

VERA: You can whip it up in a flash. I'll "like" and re-share to my follower base.

MICHAL: Me too! As long as it's not too political, you know.

VERA: The people dislike too much resistance. Just a pinch of passion, a smidge of stimulation to taste, and then an overflow of cute, quirky pictures. You could call it "Fran of the House" – like man of the house? Obviously, you'd need a house ... So what about "Fran and Friends?" Obviously, you'd need some friends ... But wait – we're your friends, honey! We could be on it!

MICHAL: Duuuude, we could be on it! We could be the stars!

VERA: Follow the stars, Fran! This is a sign!

VANĚKA: Good ideas, you guys, thanks, but um, that's not really my vision –

VERA: We know, Fran. You do your sweet little ... [*Mumbles, "whatever they are"*]

MICHAL: Why not gig around in streaming service? You could do closed captions! Ka-pow!

VERA: Or time social media alerts! Buzz beep wow!
MICHAL: Or run a dope Twitter account! Read now!
VERA: That wouldn't be selling out, honey, no way. Or, not really –
VANĚKA: I know it wouldn't. Oh, um.
MICHAL: Fran. My man. Let's get real. Are you ... ?
VANĚKA: Am I what?
VERA: Seeing anyone, honey? A girlfriend? I don't mean to assume, but obviously ...
VANĚKA: Oh, uh –
VERA: You could try an app.
MICHAL [*with a wink*]: We love indulging those before the "main meal."
VERA: You can put yourself out there without ever leaving your flat! An app! Get one today!
VANĚKA: Who ... Are you talking to me?
VERA: My followers, Fran! And Siri. They're always lending their ears. Isn't that comforting?
MICHAL: Isn't that easy?
VERA: You can get one today!
MICHAL: Do you have one today?
VANĚKA: A flat? Or ... a lover? No, no, I–I don't. Neither. None. I'm focusing on my writing currently.
[MICHAL *and* VERA *share a blatantly worried glance*]
MICHAL [*totally earnestly, albeit intending the sexual innuendo*]: Fran. Don't you wanna meet mindful "*meats*" who are massively minimalist?
VANĚKA: I'm a vegetarian.
MICHAL: Dude, why didn't you say so?! Then all you have to do is hit up –
VANĚKA: Hot yoga ... ?
VERA: *Hot yoga!* Yes! Girl! You absolutely, totally must give it your adorably sincere old college try. We're obsessed with your health, honey.
MICHAL: We care about downward-fucking dog.
VERA: We're downright devoted to it! It's a home base you can always return to throughout your cycles, like a flat. You just ... lay down flat –

THE PEOPLE'S TOAST | *Ellis Stump*

MICHAL: Most classes we spend, instead of trying other positions, entirely in downward dog.

VERA: And shavasana. That's called corpse pose.

MICHAL: In hot yoga, you end every session with corpse pose.

VERA: Fran, what's your end pose, honey, and step-by-step sequence preceding it?

VANĚKA: Oh, um, I've actually been focusing on the present, currently –

MICHAL: Fran. My man. We're so sorry to hear that.

VERA: All of us, honey, especially our Siri. She just began crying, can't you hear? We'll tend to her shortly, but you are our first-and-foremost priority. Because if you can't care for yourself, how can you expect to care for your Siri?

MICHAL: We're obsessed with your health, Fran.

VERA: We're in love with hot yoga. And – oh my god – we can teach it to you right now!

VANĚKA: What? Um, thanks, but, you don't have to –

MICHAL: Dude! We absolutely, totally must.

VERA: Dog. ASAP. You'll be obsessed with it.

[VERA *and* MICHAL *help* VANĚKA *bend over and pose, erotically and ridiculously. They can ad lib lines of motivation, and she of hesitance. Eventually, enter* ALEK, *puffing on a cigarette with his characteristic, sloshy pitcher of beer*]

ALEK: Fran, little lady, come on! The side salads need tossed! The utensils need folded in napkins! The napkin salads want folded! The side utensils want tossed! The coffee *machine needs fixed!*

[*Beat. The overgenerous Gen-Zers and middling Millennial freeze. The Boomer takes in the sight. After a moment, he scoffs*]

ALEK: Millennials. *Legrační.*

THE END

Lidovy pripitek

[VANĚKA *procházka do restaurace. Nyní, je sebejistý. Podnikání soustředěný. Ona nosí oblečení na jógu. Ona sedí, a ihned ona se vytahuje její přenosný počítač. Zklamaný, volá ona*]

Ellis Stump | THE PEOPLE'S TOAST

VANĚKA: Promiňte. Ahoj? Pane vrchni? [*Naštvaný, arogantní*] Ó můj bože, zveřejním hrozná recenze z toho okoralý, starý, zařízení. "Establishment." A já mám publikum na Internetu, větší než černá díra. říkáš ty jsi si trendy kavárna, ale očividně, byl jsi tady na 100 let!

[ALEK *vstoupí*]

ALEK: Ahoj, madam. To mi je líto nechal jsem tě čekat. Je mi to moc líto. Budu vařit cokoliv chceš, a přinesu to tobě co nejrychleji. Co ti můžu přinést?

VANĚKA [*vážný*]: Budu mít "Wifi Speciální" a jeden vanilkový karamelový moka se sójovým mlékem a čokoládovými spirálami a extra pěnou navrchu. Skim. Taky, chci plátek vašeho avokádový toast. Mletý, podobný kaše. V misce.

ALEK: Rovnou, madam.

VANĚKA: A Wifi heslo? Jaké je to slovo?

ALEK: Ach. Ano. Běžet.

VANĚKA: Promiňte?

ALEK: Heslo je: Běžet. Jako v, šéf říká: Běžet ... Staré přísloví. Nevadí.

VANĚKA: Dobře ...

ALEK: Promiňte, madam. Děkuju, madam.

[ALEK *východy.* VANĚKA *typy zuřivě na jejím počítači, nebo ona fotí z restaurace. Ale pak, najednou ...*]

PHONE: Pokračuj v chůzi.

VANĚKA: Co ... ?

PHONE: Neudělal jsi přijet u vašeho destinace. Pokračuj v chůzi. Neudělal jsi přijet u vašeho ... [*Hlas slábnout, zkreslené, jake telefon zemře*]

VANĚKA [*zírá na to*]: Hovno. Mrtvý. Ach, dobře.

[*S povzdechem,* VANĚKA *popadne nabíječku telefonu. Připojí svůj telefon k notebooku. Zatímco dobíjí se,* VANĚKA *posouvá vpřed, bez emocí. Ona lže dolů na podlaze, na jejích zádech – mrtvolná póza – a ona kouří od a Juul*]

Sex Ed for Mom

Laurie Tanner

Cast

CLAIRE: a middle-aged woman, recently separated, lonely
STEVE TUNA: Claire's mysterious date. He has a slight stutter. The actor playing STEVE should create the stutter in a way that is natural, and that does not excessively slow down the pace of the dialogue. The stuttering in the written dialogue is meant only as an indication
HONEY: VO only or projected on screen, CLAIRE's well-meaning if mischievous daughter.

Setting

Claire's home in a condo. The living room. The set can be as simple as a couch with a small coffee table and whatever else can be used to make it appear to be a living room.

[CLAIRE *is on a Facetime call with* HONEY. HONEY *can be a VO or projected video*]
CLAIRE: It's fine that I'm alone for my birthday. Don't you worry.
HONEY: Well, last year your birthday sucked …
CLAIRE: It did. Your dad had just left … then Cheshire passed … his last purr just about broke my heart.
HONEY: It was a good thing, Mom. You were always allergic to cats.
CLAIRE: Bye-bye, antihistamines!
HONEY: Mom, I can tell when you're sad. You need company –
CLAIRE: So come on over!
HONEY: Not that kind of company … besides, I have a date – I should get you a dog … how about a dog, Mom? Just kidding. What you really need is –
[*Sound of a doorbell ringing*]
CLAIRE: Don't know who that could be –

HONEY: Oh hey, you've got company – bye, Mom!
CLAIRE: No, but I wasn't expecting –
HONEY: Bye, Mom! Talk to you soon! You won't be lonely tonight!
CLAIRE: What – they left! [*Doorbell rings again. She approaches door*] What the – ? Who is it?
STEVE [*off stage*]: Hello, I'm your d-d-date.
CLAIRE [*not opening door*]: There's some mistake here. I don't have a –
STEVE: Your daughter s-sent me.
CLAIRE: I was just talking to her. She mentioned a dog, not a –
STEVE: May I come in?
CLAIRE: Wait a minute – [*looks through peephole*] who are you?
STEVE: S-Steve. I'm Steve. And you are Claire –
CLAIRE: Steve what?
STEVE: S-Steve T-t-tuna.
CLAIRE: Sounds fishy to me. What's my daughter's name?
STEVE: Honey. I can show you my ID-D – ID.
CLAIRE: You could be anyone – a random killer.
STEVE: They d-d-do say I have killer looks.
CLAIRE: Wise guy. Not sure I like that either. Are you a friend of Honey's?
STEVE: Not exactly. She hired me from I-D-D-Dates.
CLAIRE: Never heard of it.
STEVE: I'll put my card through the mail s-slot.
CLAIRE [*retrieving the card*]: Never seen one like this before.
STEVE: They're new. Also – Honey t-told me to t-tell you she has a mole on her neck, on the left.
CLAIRE: Hmm. [*Opens door cautiously. Steve steps in*] Huh! It's true about the looks.
STEVE [*gives her a bouquet*]: These are for you.
CLAIRE: Something's off here. You're too good to be true! Young enough to be my so–
STEVE: I'm ageless. Looks-s are an illusion.
CLAIRE: A philosopher, too, huh? My looks are all too real, sadly ...
STEVE: I th-think you're aes-th-thetically pleasing.
CLAIRE: How – flattering. If not romantic. Well, come in – unless you're a serial killer ...

SEX ED FOR MOM | *Laurie Tanner*

STEVE: I d-d-don't believe so.

CLAIRE: That's a relief! Take a seat. Would you like a drink–cookies–crackers–cheese?

STEVE: No thank you. I'd like you to t-t-tell me all about yourself.

CLAIRE: Really. You tell me – do they pay you well?

STEVE: Pay me? I d-d-don't understand ... I d-don't get paid.

CLAIRE: So. Not a gigolo. How does it work then?

STEVE: I'm here to keep you company, s-satisfy all your needs – and – make you laugh.

CLAIRE: Mmmm. What do you get out of it?

STEVE: I fulfill my p-purpose. And you are hap-hap-py.

CLAIRE: Curious ... that stutter ... is it random, or ... ?

STEVE: Just a few s-s-sounds. I can mostly keep it under control.

CLAIRE: I see. Not to worry. We can talk about things that don't require those sounds, if you want.

STEVE: Impossible. They're s-some of the most common s-s-sounds in the English language. If it d-d-doesn't bother you t-too much ... it won't bother me.

CLAIRE: I'm fine. What bothers me is – if this is a date – why aren't you eating or drinking? Because you're on the job?

STEVE: No! I'm just your d-date. I can d-d-dance, if you like.

CLAIRE: Ohhh? Well, that might be fun. But you're too young ... Look. Tell my kid thanks, but –

STEVE: Did you know th-that women who start d-dating again within a year of a s-separation gain increased self-confidence? Also, dating younger men contributes to their s-s-sense of s-self-worth. You have a great s-smile. Personally, I'd like to see that s-s-smile more often.

CLAIRE: My husband was always telling me to smile more.

STEVE: Th-there's a d-difference between a s-smile put on for show and a genuinely happy expression of contentment. Did being with your husband make you h-happy?

CLAIRE: It did at first ... for many years. But then he started cheating. Became more and more critical – of me, anyway. Do you mind? [*Pulls out joint or vape pen*]

STEVE: No.

CLAIRE: Do you want some?

STEVE: Show me how.

CLAIRE: Just inhale, hold it for a second – and exhale. Like that.
STEVE: Let me t-try. [*He copies her actions*]
CLAIRE: Strange. You didn't choke. Everyone chokes the first time.
STEVE: Ch-chokes?
CLAIRE: The smoke – tickles your lungs.
STEVE: Can it t-tickle si-silico-cone? My lungs are made of silicone.
CLAIRE: Why? Were they replaced?
STEVE: They should be replaced every five years or earlier, d-d-depending on usage.
CLAIRE: I had no idea prosthetics were that far advanced –
STEVE: My heart, on the other hand – well, it confuses the engineers. It sh-should have expired by now, but it's s-still going strong ...
CLAIRE: Engineers ... So – you're bionic?
STEVE: Not t-too much "bio" about me. I'm afraid. They made me pretty much from sy-synthetics.
CLAIRE: What?
STEVE: Heat-s-sensitized rubber composite, and –
CLAIRE: Oh my god – Are you saying – ? You're a – ro – !
STEVE [*faster*]: – biodegradable, compostable p-plastics made from food waste, created in Italy.
CLAIRE: A good reason to not use the garbage disposal.
STEVE: P-parts of me are made from a combination of p-platinum and p-paper ash, which is highly flexible, while being very s-strong. Now you know.
CLAIRE: Steve! *You're a robot* [*Phone rings. Claire checks who it is*] Hello, Honey? How's my evening going? *Did you just send me a robot – as a date??* ... What were you thinking? You've got a lot of nerve – listen – I'm not "getting any" what? How would you know that? Is it your business? Have you lost your mi – give him a chance?! Tell me you aren't serious – Honey? She hung up. Kids ... [*to Steve*] What are you??
STEVE: They call me AHI – Alt-t-ernative to Human Int-teraction. That's why they call me S-Steve T-Tuna. You know – Ahi Tuna? But I'm not a cold fish!
CLAIRE [*laughs in spite of herself. Beat*]: Whoah! This is crazy! When were you going to tell me?

SEX ED FOR MOM | *Laurie Tanner*

STEVE: If you didn't figure it out, I would have had to show you a video outlining my construction and purpose.

CLAIRE: At least I spared myself that. I still can't believe this –

STEVE: They th-thought it would be safer. For your d-date. I mean – s-safer for you, and for the d-d – .

CLAIRE: What did she think I'd do to a real date? Eat him alive?

STEVE: No. I d-don't – .

CLAIRE: I'm in shock. You should go!

STEVE: They did specify that I should be p-prepared for rejection.

CLAIRE: Ho ho, really? I guess rejection doesn't bother you though …

STEVE: Why would you say that?

CLAIRE: Well, it's not like you have feelings, right?

STEVE: Not really … but I'll be retired, repurposed, or d-d-disassembled for p-parts, if I can't please.

CLAIRE: But the stutter – ! That's weird. Such a human trait –

STEVE: The women engineers who designed me wanted to make me seem less p-perfect. They think the lack of p-perfection appeals to older women.

CLAIRE: It sure made me less skeptical!

STEVE: There was a small discount because of it. You could probably re-p-program me to get rid of it.

CLAIRE: But I'm not going to keep you. Such a young model – Honey must think I'm a cougar!

STEVE: No, I d-d-don't think that's it – She said your ex-husband re-married – s-someone much younger –

CLAIRE: True … barely out of her training bra. She's real though … no offense, but I miss the sex …

STEVE: No problem, Claire. I'm p-programmed to make love 365 d-different ways, inclusive of the 64 p-positions of the *Kama Sutra* – th-that's all that the less expensive models have. Your kids opted for me: s-state-of-the-art, with advanced ca-carnal knowledge.

CLAIRE: No shit! But dates aren't just about sex –

STEVE: I've been t-trained according to the philosophical and ethical t-texts of the *Kama Sutra*. In a very large book, there's just one s-section about s-sex. Most of the book underlines the importance of p-pleasing women in many different ways, not just physical. I d-don't want to flex too much, but I've had some very s-satisfied customers ... s-something to Yelp about!

CLAIRE: A sex machine with a sense of humor!

STEVE: Even S-siri can make you laugh these d-days ...

CLAIRE: After the past year, humor is ... essential. Three hundred and sixty-five ... wowww. Different sex every day of the year ...

STEVE: You can switch it up. Or if there's a groove you like –

CLAIRE: I can replay it?? This is too good to be true! The catch?

STEVE: It used to be that you had to sh-sshare me, but since the pa-pa-pan-d-d-demic – well, it isn't sa-sanitary.

CLAIRE: So – how long would I have you for, if I were to go along?

STEVE: For a week. You ca-can extend, or – If you really like me, there's a lease-to-buy option ...

CLAIRE: What if I really, really like you?

STEVE: Not s-sure I get what –

CLAIRE: If I fall in love with you. It would be unrequited, right?

STEVE: My t-training won't allow me to reject or d-dump you, and I'm very respectful. I'll only argue if you want me t-to – I'm very obedient ... I'll leave if you s-say so. But you won't fall in love with me. I'm just a t-transitional phase.

CLAIRE: Not too shabby, while I'm between real dates ... How do we go for a test drive?

STEVE: I warm up well with music ... [*Activates salsa or other music on his body*] I'm a great da-dan-n-n-dancer too.

[*Claire and Steve dance*]

CLAIRE: Mmmm ... your, uh, skin is warm ...

STEVE: It's a reaction to yours ... [*in a sexy voice*] from my s-subcutaneous sssensors.

CLAIRE [*turned on*]: Oooh ... – [*CLAIRE's phone rings. She glances at it*] Look who's calling – [*she hangs up*] later, Honey! Which position should we start with?

STEVE: *Kama Sutra* Number 8 is the Rocking Boat. Or we can try my version: the Rocking Robot! [*They laugh*]

THE END

SEX ED FOR MOM | *Laurie Tanner*

Educazione sessuale per la mamma

[*CLAIRE e HONEY stanno chiacchierando su Facetime. HONEY puo' essere una voce pre-registrata oppure una proiezione video*]
CLAIRE: Va benissimo che sono da sola per il mio compleanno. Non ti preoccupare.
HONEY: Mah. L'anno scorso il tuo compleanno fu un disastro ...
CLAIRE: E' vero. Tuo padre mi aveva appena lasciato ... poi e' passato il povero Cheshire ... le sue ultime fuse mi hanno spezzato il cuore ...
HONEY: Pero' menomale, Mamma. Sei sempre stata allergica ai gatti.
CLAIRE: Arrivederci, antistaminici!
HONEY: Mamma, riconosco sempre la tua tristezza. Hai bisogno di compagnia –
CLAIRE: E allora vieni!
HONEY: Ma non quel tipo di compagnia ... comunque, stasera esco con qualcuno. Dovrei ottenere un cane per te ... che dici, vuoi un cane, Mamma? Dai, scherzo! In realta' hai bisogno di –
[*Suona il campanello di casa*]
CLAIRE: Ma chi puo' essere –
HONEY: Dai, hai ospiti – ciao, Mamma!
CLAIRE: No, pero' non aspettava –
HONEY: Ciao, Mamma! A presto!! Non sarai sola stasera!
CLAIRE: Che cosa – Ha riattaccato! [*Il campanello insiste. CLAIRE va verso la porta*] Che diavolo – ? Chi e'?
STEVE [*fuori palco*]: B-buona sera, sono qua p-p-per il nostro appuntamento – .
CLAIRE [*senza aprire la porta*]: C'e' stato un errore. Non ho fissato – .
STEVE: Tua f-f-figlia mi hai mandato.
CLAIRE: Parlavo ora con lei. Ha riferito un cane, non un – .
STEVE: Posso entrare?
CLAIRE: Aspetta – [*guarda attraverso la spia*] chi sei?
STEVE: S-Steve. Sono Steve. E tu sei Claire –
CLAIRE: Steve cosa?
STEVE: S-Steve T-t-tuna.

CLAIRE: Mah. Per me, sa di pesce. Come si chiama mia figlia?
STEVE: Honey. P-p-posso mostrarti la mia carte d-d-d'identita.
CLAIRE: Puoi essere chuinque – un killer qualsiasi.
STEVE: D-d-dicono che ho l'aspetto di un ammazza-donne.
CLAIRE: Spiritoso, anche troppo. Sei un amico di Honey?
STEVE: Non esattamente. Mi ha trovato su il sito I-D-D-Dates.
CLAIRE: Mai sentito di questo.
STEVE: P-p-passo la mia carta nel buco per la p-posta.
CLAIRE [*guardando la carta*]: Mai visto una come questa.
STEVE: Il disegno e' nuovo. Senti un p-po' – Honey mi ha detto di dirti che ha un neo sul collo, dalla parte sinistra.
CLAIRE: Hmm. [*Apre la porta con cautela. Steve entra*] Ahh! E' vero, sei belloccio.
STEVE [*porge un mazzo di fiori*]: Questi sono per te.
CLAIRE: C'e' qualcosa che non va. Sei giovanissimo! Giovane abbastanza di essere mio figl – .
STEVE: Sono senza eta'. La bellezza e' solo un'illusione.
CLAIRE: Un filosofo addirittura? Il mio aspetto e' troppo reale, per sfortuna ...
STEVE: P-p-penso che sei esteticamente gratificante.
CLAIRE: Che lusingheria. Anche se non molto romantico. Beh, entra, entra- almeno che non sei un killer di serie ...
STEVE: C-c-credo di no.

Ana's Pictures: A Short Comedy on Nostalgia

Otilia Vieru-Baraboi

Cast

ANA: 36 years old, an interior designer, works for her own small business "World Accents"; she is an alien resident of uncertain origin (the audience must be left wondering where she is from because of her accent)

JOE: in his forties, a schoolteacher, came to the USA very young, of mixed race, ANA's husband

SEBASTIAN: ten years old, ANA and JOE's son

JOHN: 53 years old, a software engineer; ANA and JOE's new neighbor

CHORUS: disembodied children's voices.

Setting

A house in Seattle, during the first months of the global pandemic. The play starts with a chorus that defines "nostalgia."

Act 1. Scene 1

CHORUS [*disembodied children's voices read a definition of nostalgia from a dictionary of etymologies; the text is projected on a screen located in the middle of the stage*]: Nostalgia comes from Greek *algos* meaning "pain, grief, distress" and *nostos* or "homecoming." By the mid-1700s, the French term *nostalgie* is used in medical army manuals. [*Pause, instrumental tune, flute*] Noted in the eighteenth century, in references to the Swiss army soldiers, it is considered a fatal disease, especially when combined with other wounds and afflictions. [*Pause, instrumental tune, drums*] Noted in the nineteenth century, the term was used to describe any intense homesickness, as experienced by sailors, convicts, enslaved Africans, etc. [*Pause, instrumental tune, violin*] In 1867, in the *Sanitary Memoirs of the War*, the US

Otilia Vieru-Baraboi | ANA'S PICTURES: A SHORT COMEDY ON NOSTALGIA

Sanitary Commission describes nostalgia as a serious medical problem in the American Civil War: there were reported 2588 cases of nostalgia and thirteen deaths from this cause. [*Pause, instrumental tune, drums*]

Scene 2

[ANA's *home office, she's sitting at her desk, facing the audience; her face is barely distinguishable thanks to the dim light coming from the monitor. She is looking through some pictures, stopping and typing things from time to time. At some point she stops – a black-and-white picture is projected behind her on the screen. The image is small and blurry at first – it becomes bigger and clearer as the audience hears* ANA's *voice describing it*]

ANA [*she has a slight undistinguishable accent – not British, Russian, French, etc. – it should not be traced to any specific culture or location; the actor should record herself*]: I'm holding your hand, my skirt is so short, it looks more like a saggy second-hand tutu. On the left, a stuffed giant bear defies the hunter, frozen in time, his front paws raised up in a menacing pose, its teeth sharpened by the fear of all the kids who have their picture taken besides this monumental relic. In its rotten heart, honey has turned into an empty amber container. You look proud of your brave little girl; her short haircut and pale cuteness remind you of the boy you always wanted. It was our last family vacation, things just kept on going down the drain after that summer. We stopped taking pictures. Don't we all want to document moments of bliss only?

[*The phone rings, she picks up promptly, her voice sounds surprisingly cheerful*]

ANA: Hi there, so glad you called. I was looking for the right finishing touches for your living room. The colors are predominantly *hygge*, which can be monotone also – you need a few accent pieces to give you that sense of earthy warmth and global savviness you are looking for. Yes, yes ... Don't worry, we won't alter in any way the mid-century modern vibe of the remodel. Accent pieces are always about measure and balance. The two of us have developed a relationship by now, you need to trust me with this. Ok, yes ... sure. I can arrange a virtual tour of that gallery. I must warn you, though: it's not going to be cheap, they support fair trade and local designers ... but you would be doing the right thing supporting their business. Just like everyone, if not more, they've been hit hard because of transportation delays, among other things ... All right, I understand, I would do the same. We're living in such uncertain times. Let's look at their offer and keep our options open ... Yes, sure. Have a nice day, talk to you later, enjoy your walk. [*She hangs up; when she mentions the word "hygge," images of white, gray, and black interiors with many house plants and natural light are projected onto the screen in the backdrop décor*] You spoiled brat! You really think you own everyone, don't you ... [*Someone knocks at the door, but doesn't come in*]

SEBASTIAN: Mom, Moooom! Can I come in? I need to tell you something! It's important! Mom, we really need to call Kyle's mom and ask her for a playdate at the park. I just got the new LEGO set. Found it on the porch this morning! Please, please, we'll be careful, we'll keep our distance and masks on. I promise I'll keep my nose tucked in inside. I really need to see him today. He's been waiting for you to call his mom. Will you please do it? I just want to make sure he knows my set got here first. Can you please text his mom? Please, mom, Pleeeeeaaaazzzz. Mom!

ANA [*raising her voice*]: Sebastian, how many times have I told you not to come knocking at my door if it's closed? That means I'm busy working. I understand you're impatient, but can you wait till we eat lunch? Aren't you supposed to be in school? Don't make me come out, you'll be in big trouble. Go back to your room.

SEBASTIAN: Mom, we're taking a short break. Otherwise, you wouldn't be talking to me right now. Can you please text his mom? You have her phone number, don't you?

[*The phone rings again, ANA picks up*]

ANA: Yes, this is Ana speaking. Hello?! [*No one speaks. ANA waits two seconds and hangs up*]

Scene 3

[*In the same house, in the kitchen. ANA and JOE are having a conversation. JOE is cutting vegetables, ANA is looking through a pile*

Otilia Vieru-Baraboi | ANA'S PICTURES: A SHORT COMEDY ON NOSTALGIA

of mail. They share a bottle of red wine. The kitchen has earthy tones, a Turkish kilim runner on the floor, art on the walls, hand-painted ceramic plates from across the globe, paintings of food and flowers, and an unusual wool mask with a big mouth open wide and teeth made out of white beans. Plants everywhere. A colorful, lived-in space, in contrast with the white kitchens, trendy in architecture magazines and real estate staging]

JOE: I'm exhausted. I just spent 30 min trying to convince him it's not a good idea.

ANA: You bet, bringing here 40 exchange students from overseas is a really bad idea right now. For one, you won't find any host families, and second, I bet their own parents won't let them travel.

JOE: You'd be surprised, I just heard of a group of teens from Saint Peter's who went on a trip to Marrakesh organized by the school – two of them got sick and they all needed to quarantine for the entire time. So here you go! How insane can teachers and parents be? It's not the kids' fault. I'm telling you, we live in an upside down world! Some grown-ups should not be allowed to raise kids.

ANA: I know, I get your point. But let's not exaggerate. You don't know all the details. Hmm. Should we make our regular dish to welcome the new neighbors?

JOE: I honestly don't think so, everyone is getting a bit paranoid about sharing food these days.

ANA: Ah, what am I thinking? You're right. I wouldn't eat anybody's food right now. There's got to be a different way to show they're welcome here. Besides, just bringing food once won't make any difference. We even got a welcome party and what for, exactly? We never became close to anyone, everyone just minds their own business. We could all die one day, none of our neighbors will notice, I'm telling you.

JOE: You're so dramatic. But that's what I love the most about you! [*He stops whatever he is doing and reaches out to give her a kiss. They're obviously happy, there is nothing mechanical or rushed in this spontaneous gesture of affection*]

ANA'S PICTURES: A SHORT COMEDY ON NOSTALGIA | *Otilia Vieru-Baraboi*

ANA: Hmm, look who's talking. We must have been twins in a past life. Remember that time when you ... [*She is cut short by* SEBASTIAN *who comes in the room, running*]

SEBASTIAN: Dad, did you text Kyle's mom? I really need to tell Kyle I got the LEGO set today.

JOE: We need to eat dinner first. Why don't you set the table? Remember your rewards? Setting the table is worth a lot of points! Right, mom?

ANA: Oh, yeah! I'll write it down, if you do it. You need to save money for the cool *Star Wars* LEGO you showed me.

SEBASTIAN: Arhhh, this is exactly what you told me at lunch time! You guys are stalling. Why won't you do this one little thing for me?

[*As* SEBASTIAN *sets the table, pungent smells are starting to emanate from the big pot where* JOE *was dropping all the vegetables. As they sit down to eat, one can hear the muffled sounds of a cheerful conversation, and an instrumental jazzy tune with Balkan/manouche influences on the background*]

Scene 4

[*The kitchen décor gets squished into the right side of the stage. There is a covered plate on the table. On the left side we have one bed, a nightstand and a window through which we can see a full red moon.* JOE *doesn't move, he snores from time to time.* ANA *speaks in her sleep*]

ANA: Lines. Everything. Empty milk bottles. Oranges. Green bananas. Canned fruit. Meat. Oh, Lord Almighty! Chicken wings and feet. Sour cherry jam for the guests. Polenta with sugar for deserts. Kent cigarettes and coffee beans for the doctors' bribe. Coffee smells so good ... Hmmm ... I wish I had a cup of that coffee one day, from that exact same coffee bag. Those damn doctors, they always took the coffee and Kent cigarettes, but they never fixed mom. Never ever ... Christmas carols. Dances. The masked dancers are coming!!! Stay indoors, they like to scare the kids!

Otilia Vieru-Baraboi | ANA'S PICTURES: A SHORT COMEDY ON NOSTALGIA

[*Her sleep becomes more and more agitated. At the same time, in the kitchen, a man wearing a real bear fur suit eats the food from the table ravenously, making inarticulate sounds*]

ANA [*continues to speak in her sleep*]: I love the bear dances; they chase the evil spirits away. I wish they made the grizzlies dance here. We would all be happier, if they made the wolves and the bears dance with the mountain goats.

[JOE *wakes up, startled, looks at Ana and starts to shake her up*]

JOE: Ana, wake up, you're talking in your sleep again. And what the heck, I think there is someone downstairs!

[*As soon as he says this and* ANA *wakes up, disheveled, the bear disappears from the kitchen.* JOE *goes to the kitchen and sees no one is there. On his way out back to the bedroom, he notices someone has eaten the food left on a plate on the table.* ANA *joins him*]

ANA: What's going on here, Joe?

JOE: I've no idea ... It looks like someone ate our leftovers.

ANA: It couldn't have been Sebastian, he hates tagine with *mămăligă*!

JOE: I told you we should have made couscous!

ANA: Besides, he's sound asleep and would never come down here in the middle of the night since we let him watch *Stranger Things*.

JOE: Yeah, he sees the Demogorgon everywhere now. We shouldn't have let him watch this show. I told you it's not for kids his age.

ANA: Oh, will you give me a break with this, please? All the kids in his class are watching it. You should see their chat conversations. Anyways, what's done is done!

JOE: Yes, but their parents will think we started it. They always blame him for starting everything. They think we're bad parents.

ANA: Seriously, are we going to talk about it now? Everyone is a bit xenophobic in this great liberal city.

JOE: One more reason for us to make an effort. After all, we're the newcomers here.

ANA: The real dangerous monsters are the dormant ones. The pandemic just woke them up. They would have banned us all from the city, if this was in the Middle Ages.

JOE: Will you stop being so melodramatic, so, so ... this is pure paranoia!

ANA'S PICTURES: A SHORT COMEDY ON NOSTALGIA | *Otilia Vieru-Baraboi*

ANA: Yes, you're right, paranoia is my second nature. I was born in the Balkans, what do you expect? Betrayal is in our mothers' milk! And now, can you please find a valid explanation for the noises you heard in the kitchen and the fact that someone did eat our tagine?

JOE: I'm going to check the door and windows, see if there are any traces of a break-in. I'm afraid we cannot call the police for this. It'd be ridiculous: "Hey, Mr. Officer, someone broke into our house in the middle of the night and ate our *mămăligă* with tagine!" Is this even a crime? The poor guy, whoever that was, must have been starving!

[*As JOE goes outside, ANA exits the kitchen and goes back into the bedroom. She starts checking out messages on her phone, her face somehow deformed under the light of the screen*]

ANA: Damn it, what a crazy spoiled bitch! Where should I find kilims from Afghanistan in two weeks?

[*The décor changes on the other side of the stage. The kitchen is replaced by Joe and Ana's back yard*]

Scene 5

[*JOHN is in his fifties, completely bald and dressed in his Hanna Andersson striped PJs. JOE finds their neighbor John sitting outside on their porch*]

JOE: Dear God, John! You gave me quite a scare! What are you doing here? Is everything all right?

JOHN: What the heck! You scared me, too! What are you doing outside in the middle of the night?

JOE: Well, to start with, this happens to be my yard. You're on my property, man! Second, I thought I heard someone downstairs in my kitchen, and guess what! Someone was inside my kitchen! Ate our leftovers from the kitchen table.

JOHN: Is that so? That sounds crazy! Reminds me of a distorted version of Goldilocks. [*He laughs like a mad person. JOE looks at him puzzled*] I woke up thinking someone's in my kitchen, too. [*Continues to laugh*] Then I'm pretty damn sure I heard a growl,

Otilia Vieru-Baraboi | ANA'S PICTURES: A SHORT COMEDY ON NOSTALGIA

like a bear's. When I went into the kitchen, all seemed fine, but *then* ... Then I found a huge crap under the island. And it stank like hell. I had to go out and take some fresh air otherwise I would have puked my insides out. I saw your lights were on and wanted to come over, desperate for help, but then I stopped because I could hear you guys yelling at each other.

JOE: Damn these wooden houses! One cannot even have a decent fight without all the neighbors knowing about it!

JOHN: What would you do? Call the police? They'll think I'm on drugs or something ...

JOE: Are you serious? This is unbelievable! I don't know why I feel we're missing something major here. Could it be that a bunch of kids decided to play tricks on us? Everyone is so bored to death these days ... I would start playing pranks on grown-ups, too! We deserve it, we created this world of mess for them! Planet Shithole! This is our legacy to them! More rules to follow, more regulations. Well, what the heck, I feel we should all take a dump somewhere forbidden, like on someone else's property, on a fancy dining table ...

JOHN: I hear you, but the new regulations are serious, it's for our own protection. Don't they have them in your country?

JOE: They do, they do. This is my country, man. We came here when I was five, remember?

JOHN: Well, yes. And still. You could be more grateful. Anyways, should we call the police, or go to bed? I still need to clean up that huge shit. The whole house stinks.

JOE: You're welcome to sleep on our couch and clean that in the morning.

JOHN: That's so nice of you. But we cannot do that. We're not allowed to go into each other's houses, remember? I'll just deal with it.

JOE: Oh, yeah, forgot about that for a second. How are we going to live through this? Well, at least the intruder or intruders were not afraid of getting the virus from us.

JOHN: What do you expect ... Desperate people act like animals.

[*They part ways*]

ANA'S PICTURES: A SHORT COMEDY ON NOSTALGIA | *Otilia Vieru-Baraboi*

Act 2. Scene 1

[*ANA's home office, she's sitting in an armchair, her legs under her, facing the audience. She is looking through a bulky picture album. The audience can see the pictures she is looking at projected on the big screen in the background of the stage*]

ANA [*we hear a recording, as if having access to her thoughts*]: In this one, I remember feeling the stag deer's fur, rough under my hesitant, wet palm. My eyes are literally popping out with fear. I was scared the worms that ate the insides of this majestic animal would come out and crawl under my nails, looking for a fresh host to inhabit. No one is holding my hand in this one, that's probably why I seem so terrified. I wonder if the picture was taken at the same time, in the same photo studio, with the one with the bear. There is no indication of the date. It looks like I'm about the same age. I don't recognize the clothes in this one. I always thought I never had beautiful velvety dresses growing up. Could it be a dress that I borrowed from the photographer? It kind of looks like a dress one would wear for a funeral, but then, one can never be sure of the color in these black-and-white pictures. All my memories are in black and white, and gray. Like all the buildings, the end-of-the-school-year pictures, the weddings, the cartoons we watched for twenty minutes on Saturdays. [*The phone rings, she picks up, sounds surprisingly happy*]

ANA: I was hoping you would call me first. I was just thinking of you, looking through a catalogue with the new trends in Scandinavian design. Have you heard of *hygge*? It comes from Danish. These Danish, they sure know how to appreciate life! It's the ultimate idea of coziness, the art of creating a space that tells you immediately "you're home now; you can relax, leave all your worries behind that gorgeous door and enjoy your spa-like bathroom, the fluffiness of your monochrome handwoven Persian rugs. Make yourself a chamomile cup of tea and read that *New Yorker* you never have the time to read, tucked into the soft embrace of your Dania sectional couch" ... Oh, but of course! It's spelled H-Y-G-G-E. Yes, you got that right. H-Y-G-G-E. It's pronounced "hoo-guh." Sorry, there is no translation into English, I'm afraid. It's a foreign import. But hey, this means

Otilia Vieru-Baraboi | ANA'S PICTURES: A SHORT COMEDY ON NOSTALGIA

it's European quality design, guaranteed! ... I understand. You prefer Martha Steward and the country cottage style. I agree, it's a more accessible and familiar form of coziness. I'll gather a few magazines and bring them to your house. No need to answer the door, I'll leave them on your porch. I've got a runny nose, nothing bad. Not COVID, thank God, just got a negative test. I just don't want to spread it around. I'm sooo excited to work on your second remodel, I totally see your vision. It's going to be clean, colorful, warm, welcoming, American. [*Ana hangs up*] Thank God, for COVID! I don't need to see my clients all the time. It's so hard to set up boundaries. They all feel compelled to take out their family albums when I visit ...

[*Someone knocks at the door, but doesn't come in*]

SEBASTIAN: Mom, Moooom! Can I come in? I need to tell you something! It's important! Mom, can you please ...

ANA [*stands up and opens the door*]: Yes, can't you see I'm working? God, how hard can it be for you to understand?

SEBASTIAN: Mom, you promised you'll do something about it and so far, nothing's changed. Can you talk to the principal? I didn't do anything bad. She closed the chat for no reason whatsoever. And now, how are we supposed to talk to each other? You won't get me a phone ... All my friends have one.

ANA: Sebi, we talked about it numerous times. Not all your friends have a phone. Dear God, I cannot believe we're having this conversation again! You need to be more appreciative of the things you already have. You don't need a phone, it's bad for you. Your brain is not developed yet, and there are a ton of scientific studies showing the magnetic waves can cause damage to your head. Phones are bad for grown-ups, too. And besides, this is not the issue here. You guys were disrupting the class with that chat feature. It's one thing to use it during the breaks, but you were using it all the time. The teachers complained. The principal didn't just decide on her own. Look, I know it's hard for you and you miss playing with your friends. I'm really sorry we are going through this and it's taking so long. Who would have thought?

[*The phone rings again. ANA picks up. SEBASTIAN takes her seat in the green armchair*]

ANA'S PICTURES: A SHORT COMEDY ON NOSTALGIA | Otilia Vieru-Baraboi

ANA: Yes, this is Ana speaking. It should have arrived by now. I made the order a month ago and they had the peach color in stock. Yes, I'm aware it's getting harder and harder to get supplies now, but you shouldn't lie to your clients. We signed the papers, I paid for everything. Look, I don't want to settle for new delivery date. I want my money back now! You're ruining my business.

SEBASTIAN: Mom, can you please take care of it after you're done with this call?

ANA [covers the phone with her hand]: Sebastian, you're grounded! How many times do I have to tell you to stop asking for things when I'm on the phone?

SEBASTIAN: But, mom!

ANA: I don't want to hear it! Go back to your room! We'll talk later.

[Sebastian leaves the room, slamming the door hard]

ANA: Sorry about that. I needed to take care of something urgent. Hello? Hello? Unbelievable! He hanged on me.

[ANA sits back into her armchair, takes the photo album, but doesn't turn the pages. She keeps her eyes closed. Her phone starts to ring, but she doesn't pick up]

Scene 2

[Nighttime. ANA's home office décor gets squished into the right side of the stage. On the left side of the stage, ANA and JOE's bedroom. JOE snores from time to time. ANA reads her phone messages. She hears a noise outside, like someone banged the gate hard. She jumps out of bed and goes by the window. Checks out the yard cautiously, trying not to show herself. She doesn't see anything, but the noises don't stop, resembling to an animal's bleating]

ANA: Joe, you should go out in the yard and check out who there. I'm pretty sure there's some sort of animal.

JOE: [half asleep] Oh, no. I'd rather not do that, what if I get attacked?

ANA: No, you won't. I'll come with you. Or let's call the police, tell them someone's trespassing.

JOE: I'm not sure they'll come if we cannot describe the suspect.

ANA: But we haven't seen the suspect!

Otilia Vieru-Baraboi | ANA'S PICTURES: A SHORT COMEDY ON NOSTALGIA

JOE: Exactly!
ANA: Let's go take a look at the suspect!
JOE: I'm not sure there's one ...
ANA: Joe, stop stalling, put your slippers on and follow me. Or would you'd rather let me go alone?
JOE: Really, Ana! You're forcing me to come with you. I wouldn't let you go on your own. What if there's some kind of coyote out there. People have spotted some near the Arboretum.
ANA: We need to do something. We cannot just go back to sleep.
JOE: Ok, all right. I'm coming. Let me put on some joggers. I cannot just go out in my pajamas.
ANA: All right, but hurry up. I'll put on some jeans, too.
[SEBASTIAN *barges in as they get dressed*]
SEBASTIAN: Mom, dad, there is some sort of animal in the ...
ANA and JOE: Good Lord, Sebastian! You scared us! Where did you see it?
SEBASTIAN: It's eating your red roses, mom.
ANA: What???
JOE: What kind of an animal? How big?
SEBASTIAN: Quite big. As big as a cow.
JOE: Does it have horns?
ANA: Stop asking questions and let's go. Sebastian, stay here.
SEBASTIAN: Why can't I come? I want to come!
ANA: No, what if it's dangerous?!
JOE: Yeah, you'd better stay inside the house. Keep my phone. If we don't come back in ten minutes, call 911.
[*Sebastian starts to cry*]
ANA: Joe, you're traumatizing the kid. Now what do we do with him?
JOE: He needs to learn, we're sheltering him too much. At his age, I was so much more aware of my surroundings. My family didn't raise me to be hopeless. He should be able to call 911, if his parents are attacked by some wild animal in the middle of the night.
ANA: Honey, please let's not overreact. I'm sure we're not in danger. It must be some big dog. Like a Great Dane or something.
JOE: Sebi said he saw an animal as big as a cow.

ANA'S PICTURES: A SHORT COMEDY ON NOSTALGIA | *Otilia Vieru-Baraboi*

SEBASTIAN [*sobbing*]: It could be a horse. What if they raise horses at the golf course near the Arboretum? Or what if some policeman's horse got lost?
[*Their conversation is interrupted abruptly by a load roar*]
JOE: What was that? [*He opens a closet and takes out a mop*]
ANA: What are you going to do with it?
JOE: A spear.
ANA: Are you serious? Let's call the police!
JOE: Not a good idea. They won't come, I'm telling you.
[*The three of them exit the stage*]

Scene 3

[*SEBASTIAN, ANA, and JOE, in the backyard. JOE is brandishing some kind of spear made from the mop to which he taped two knives. The shadow of a massive stag deer is projected on the background screen*]
JOE: Take this! For eating my wife's roses.
ANA: Joe, let the poor animal be. He is harmless, don't you see? All the plants are dead, anyway. They'll grow back in the spring. He's starving, poor thing.
SEBASTIAN: Mom, mom!!! Can someone talk to me? What kind of an animal is this? Mom, he looks like the animal in your photo album. The one you were photographed with. How can this be?
ANA: Sebi, I'm sure it's a coincidence. That animal was dead and stuffed. Besides, we don't have that type of animal here. They can only be found in the Carpathians.
SEBASTIAN: Mom, we do, there's plenty of deer in our woods.
ANA: Sebi, this animal is not a Carpathian stag deer. Look at it! It's so tiny and frail ...
SEBASTIAN: Mom, what if it's a baby? A kid?
ANA: Its horns are too big!
JOE: So what now? Do we let it eat our roses?
ANA: Yes! I don't want you to touch it in any way!
SEBASTIAN: Shouldn't we call animal protection or something?
JOE: Yes! Let's call the police!
ANA: Joe, the police don't care about animals in our yard! It's not their business to handle them.

Otilia Vieru-Baraboi | ANA'S PICTURES: A SHORT COMEDY ON NOSTALGIA

JOE: Then let's go back inside. This guy doesn't look too scary to me.
[JOHN *comes in, agitated, with a gun.* SEBASTIAN *hides behind his mother*]
ANA [*shouts, obviously scared*]: What are you doing here with a gun?
JOE [*goes between* JOHN *and his wife*]: John, back up, don't shoot, it's not dangerous, it's just eating plants!
JOHN [*shouts, aiming the gun at the stag deer*]: Don't move, grizzlies are dangerous, he'll kill all of you.
JOE: Where on Earth do you see grizzlies? You're obviously not OK! Give me the gun! You're on my property! You're trespassing!
ANA: John, please, calm down! I beg you! Sebi is with us!
SEBASTIAN [*screaming out loud*]: Mooom!!! Daaad!!!
[*When* SEBASTIAN *screams, the stag deer runs away fast and disappears in the neighbor's yard.* JOHN *runs after it, agitating his gun*]

Scene 4

[ANA, JOE, *and* SEBASTIAN *are in the kitchen*]
JOE: He was chasing a grizzly! In his head, he was defending us! He was acting in good faith!
ANA: He was totally delusional! He could have killed us all!
SEBASTIAN: Mom, dad, do we even have grizzly bears in the Pacific Northwest?
JOE: No, we don't! They have them in Montana and Idaho ... I think ...
ANA: We had brown bears where I grew up. I have a picture with one. My father had taken me to the professional photographer, I don't remember how old I was ... I do remember how frightened I was by the menagerie of stuffed animals. Taxidermy is quite a horrific craft, if you ask me ...
SEBASTIAN: Did you have to choose between other animals? Why the bear?
ANA: My father chose the bear ... I was so scared, cried a lot. He wanted me to be as brave as a boy, he kept saying ... He said we come from a family of bear hunters and I needed to keep the

ANA'S PICTURES: A SHORT COMEDY ON NOSTALGIA | *Otilia Vieru-Baraboi*

courage in my blood. Well, I guess, Sebi, you should now carry on his genes ...

JOE: Sorry, but that's so wrong! I don't agree. The old world cannot make the rules in the new world. I come from a long line of hunters, too! This doesn't mean I want my son to kill anything that moves.

SEBASTIAN: Guys, stop arguing. I would have loved to meet these old hunters.

ANA: No, I'm glad you never got to meet my father. But your father's father is a very sweet man. So, it's good you know that side of the family.

JOE: Ana, you don't really mean that. Why you're saying such things! Always so intense, so ...

ANA: Melodramatic?

JOE: Yes, yes!

ANA: What do you expect?

JOE: I know, I know ... You come from the Balkans! And that's what I love about you!

SEBASTIAN: Can we visit the Balkans?

ANA: Yes, some day ... I can show you some pictures in the meantime ... Me, with more stuffed animals, foggy mountains, black and white landscapes ... And I bet I can find some really cool and scary bear dances on YouTube ...

[*The curtain falls, as we see on the screen bear dances on tunes of drums and whistles*]

THE END

Les Photos d'Ana

Acte 1. Scène 5

[*JOHN a une cinquantaine d'années, complètement chauve, habillé en pyjamas à rayures de Hannah Andersson. JOE le trouve dehors assis sur leur terrasse*]

JOE: Ça alors, John! Vous m'avez fait peur, vous savez! Qu'est-ce que vous faites ici? Tout va bien?

JOHN: Nom de Dieu! Vous aussi, vous m'avez fait peur! Qu'est-ce que vous faites ici en pleine nuit?

JOE: Bon, pour commencer, ici c'est chez moi. C'est vous qui êtes l'intrus, pas moi! Et puis, j'ai cru entendre quelqu'un dans ma cuisine et je suis descendu voir. Et vous voulez savoir? Quelqu'un était vraiment venu nous rendre visite! Et cette personne a mangé les restes de notre diner que nous avions laissés sur la table.

JOHN: Sans blague? Mais c'est dingue! Cela me fait penser à une version pas mal déformée de Boucle d'Or. [*Il se met à rire comme un malade mental.* JOE *le regarde stupéfait*] Moi aussi, je me suis réveillé tout d'un coup, pensant qu'il y avait un intrus dans ma cuisine. [*Continue à rire*] Et puis, je suis certain avoir entendu un rugissement, on aurait dit un ours. Quand je suis allé voir dans la cuisine, tout avait l'air normal, jusqu'au moment où ... j'ai trouvé une grosse merde sous l'îlot de cuisine. Et je ne vous dis pas l'odeur ... épouvantable. Il a fallu que je sorte prendre de l'air, sinon je risquais de vomir comme pas possible. J'ai vu de la lumière chez vous, et j'ai pensé que je devrais aller vous demander de l'aide, mais j'ai changé d'avis quand je vous ai entendus vous crier dessus.

JOE: Ah, je déteste ces maisons en bois! On ne peut même pas avoir une dispute tranquille sans que les voisins l'entendent!

JOHN: Que feriez-vous à ma place? Vous pensez que je devrais appeler la police? On me prendra pour un drogué ou qui sait ...

JOE: Vous ne plaisantez pas, non? C'est quand même incroyable! Je ne sais pas pourquoi j'ai l'impression que quelque chose de très important vous échappe. Je me demande si ce ne serait une bande de sales gosses qui vous aurait joué un mauvais tour. On s'ennuie tous tellement en ce moment ... J'aurais tellement envie, moi aussi, de me mettre à faire des farces aux adultes! Nous le méritons bien, vous savez, nous avons créé ce monde plein de merdes pour eux! La Planète Trou de Merde! C'est ça, notre cadeau pour les générations à venir! Plus de règles à suivre, des règlements pour tout! Je vous le jure, je commence à penser qu'on devrait tous chier des grosses merdes dans des endroits tabous, comme dans la maison de quelqu'un, sur une table bien élégante ...

ANA'S PICTURES: A SHORT COMEDY ON NOSTALGIA | *Otilia Vieru-Baraboi*

JOHN: Je vois ce que vous voulez dire, mais les nouveaux règlements sont très sérieux, c'est pour notre protection. Il y en a pas, des règlements, dans votre pays?

JOE: Il y en a, il y en a. Mais, c'est ici mon pays. Je suis arrivé ici quand j'avais cinq ans, il me semble vous l'avoir déjà dit, non?

JOHN: Ah, bon. Tout compte fait, vous devriez vous montrer plus reconnaissant. Revenons à nos moutons. Devrions-nous appeler la police, ou aller nous coucher ? Et il ne faut pas oublier de nettoyer cette grosse merde. Ça pue partout dans la maison.

JOE: Vous pouvez dormir sur notre canapé et nettoyer tout le matin.

JOHN: C'est vraiment gentil de votre part. Mais on ne peut pas faire une chose pareille. Il est interdit d'aller dans les maisons des gens. C'est bon, je me débrouillerai tout seul.

JOE: Oh, oui, j'ai complètement oublié cette interdiction. Comment ferons-nous pour survivre dans ces conditions ? Au moins, l'intrus n'a pas eu peur d'attraper le virus chez nous.

JOHN: Que voulez-vous ... Quand les gens sont désespérés, ils se comportent comme des animaux ...

[*Ils se séparent*]

Biographies

Christine Benvenuto is the author of two works of nonfiction, *Shiksa* and *Sex Changes*, published by St. Martin's Press, and her short stories, essays, and articles have appeared in many newspapers, magazines, and anthologies. Her plays have been performed in the Boston Theater Marathon, as part of a show produced by The Braid in Los Angeles, in western Massachusetts, and online.

Barbara Blatner is a playwright, poet and composer–musician who lives with her partner in Washington Heights, Manhattan, and teaches workshops at the Hudson Valley Writers Center. During the first year of the COVID pandemic, with a dear friend, Barbara studied each line of *Hamlet* with an eye to how to direct the play.

Sarah Congress writes comedic scripts for theatre and television. Most recently, her comedy *Dracula … in Denver!* received two productions at the Shelton Theatre of San Francisco as part of the Your Worst Nightmare Play Festival (April, 2022). Her full-length play *The Angel Manual* was produced in the 2021 HB Studio Playwright's Reading Series (June, 2021) and her short play *Fresh Kills* was in the 2021 Downtown Urban Arts Festival (June, 2021). She currently serves as the Creative Content Writer for Catalia Health, and lives in Philadelphia.

Connie Dinkler resides in Salisbury, North Carolina where she runs her private counseling practice while spending her free time writing and ballroom dancing. Connie has published several poems and short stories, won two local literary awards, and has had eight ten-minute plays produced in Florida, Illinois, New York and North Carolina. Her ten-minute play, *Not a Dark and Stormy Night* was a runner-up in Clocktower Players' 2020 *Amaze* short play competition and was also included in Memoriam Development's annual horror anthology, *Nightshade* in 2021. Her full-length play *Happy Couples* was included in the New Works Virtual Festival in 2020.

Selma Dragoş is a queer mother who grew up in Romania in the 1980s reading *The Arabian Nights* as a means to learn more about her Moroccan heritage. When she realized she had her sources wrong, she decided her confusion made a very good story. She is now a children's theatre maker. When she is not writing or directing, she works with teachers, parents, and children to create playful educational experiences that further fuel her plays or theatre shows.

Tjaša Ferme is an award-winning actor, playwright, and creator and has received a Slovenian National Film Award and Stane Sever classical stage award. The Founding Artistic Director of Transforma Theatre, she created *The Female Role Model Project*, blending interactive theatre with neuroscience, premiering Off-Broadway at 3-Legged Dog and Edinburgh Fringe; the play received a NYITA nomination for Outstanding Innovative Design and Fast Company's honorary mention for World Changing Ideas Awards. In 2021 Ferme created the sold-out Science in Theatre Festival covered by Forbes and American Theatre Magazine. Tjaša is the creator of the short film *Ophelia's Flip* (Cannes Film Festival, 2012), interactive solo shows, *Wild Child in the City* and *My Marlene* (HERE), etc. https://tjasaferme.com/

Cătălina Florina Florescu was born in Romania and came to the USA 24 years ago. She holds a Ph.D. in Medical Humanities, teaches at Pace University, is the curator of New Play Festival at JCTC, and has a beautiful son. She is a published author and playwright who loves to travel. www.catalinaflorescu.com/

Avery Grace (she/they) is a queer/trans/neurodiverse, former sex worker poet–playwright currently living on the Occupied Lands of the Confederated Tribes of Warm Springs, otherwise known as Bend, Oregon. Her work is featured in: *Non-Binary: An Anthology of Gender and Identity,* and *All of Me: Stories of Love, Anger, and the Female Body.* You can find more of Avery's writing in their debut book of poetry, *Laid Bare*, and at www.averybraverygrace.com. When not writing, Avery coparents three children with their partner, and helps queer, trans, and intersex people cultivate personal pleasure and sexual/sensual authenticity as forms of liberation.

Jinna Kim is a Korean American multidisciplinary artist who initially trained in classical music and is based in North Carolina. In addition to being a SAG-AFTRA eligible actress, Jinna continues to write, produce short films, exhibit digital media, and create award-winning interdisciplinary projects. In 2021, she was an artist-in-residence at Künstlerstadt Kalbe in Germany and her first short film *Chinese Girl Wants Vote* became part of the Digital Public Library of America. In 2022, she was part of the Queen City New Play Initiative Inaugural Microplay Commission playwright cohort and separately attended the World Expo in Dubai thanks to the Arts & Science Council individual artist support grant.

Elena Naskova was born and raised in Macedonia. She immigrated to the USA when she was 25 years old. Her plays have been produced in the USA, Canada, Spain, and the UAE. She is also a published playwright and poet. Besides plays, Elena has written poetry, short stories, and haiku, and when she doesn't write, she loves to paint.

Joyce Newman Scott started college in her fifties after a successful career as an actor and a flight attendant. She studied Screenwriting at the University of Miami and Creative Writing at Florida International University. Her short stories have appeared in multiple anthologies. Her play, *The Happy Place* was a top-fifteen winner Raven Short Play Festival, California. *The Menopausal Freshman* monologue was chosen by the Burning Man Festival in the UK and published by Smith & Kraus in *The Best Women's Monologues of 2021*. She is a proud member of SAG/AFTRA and DG.

Ornella Ohayon was born and raised in Paris. She is a playwright, screenwriter, and essayist who was trained at UCLA. Her scripts have been placed in competitions in the USA and the UK, such as the Atlanta Film Festival, ScreenCraft, the Writer's Digest, the Filmmatic Comedy Awards, and the Kenneth Branagh Award at the Windsor Fringe. Ornella is bilingual and writes in both French and English. She loves traveling and meeting new people with stories to write about.

Cindi Sansone-Braff is an award-winning playwright. She has a BFA in Theatre from UCONN and is a member of the Dramatists Guild and the Long Island Authors Group. She is the author of *Grant Me a Higher Love, Why Good People Can't Leave Bad Rela-*

tionships, and *Confessions of a Reluctant Long Island Psychic*. www.grantmeahigherlove.com/

Ellis Abigail Stump (they/she) is a NYC-based Columbia University Playwriting MFA student, Barnard College adjunct professor, and Off-Broadway and internationally developed playwright from rural Lancaster County, Pennsylvania. Ellis' dark comedy *Once on Rumspringa* (Chain Theatre Residency, Ascending Playwright Award, Bay Street Finalist, American Blues Theatre Semifinalist; 2022) premiered at The Wild Project in May. Their biopic *Where I've Never Gone* (Emerson Theatre Finalist, Athena Project Finalist; 2021) runs summer 2022 at Westbeth Artist Residency. *The People's Toast* earned the Václav Havel Playwriting Award, a residency at Prague Performing Arts Academy, and productions by Bohemian National Society and University of Toronto. www.ellisstump.com/

Laurie Tanner resides near Miami, Florida. She has been writing forever, but until recently kept most of it to herself. Her plays have been produced or read at Broward College, Femuscripts, Thinking Cap Theatre, NCPLab, Naked Angels, Cutler Bay Community Theatre, Nova Theatre, PlayZoomers, and by Thru-Line Theatre Company at the Voices of Women Theatre Festival. With two other South Florida locals, she formed a theater production company, Femuscripts (because manuscripts are overdone) in 2020. Femuscripts has produced four virtual shows of short works by women, including her works. She is currently working on full-length historical plays.

Otilia Vieru-Baraboi moved to Seattle from Romania 22 years ago. She holds a Ph.D. in French Literature and studied at various universities in Romania, Switzerland, and the USA. She wrote articles on French post-colonial authors and published short fiction in Europe. Otilia is also the president and co-founder of American Romanian Cultural Society, a nonprofit that organizes a Romanian Film Festival and many other educational and cultural projects. She is currently working on a book on untranslatability.

www.ingramcontent.com/pod-product-compliance
Lightning Source LLC
Chambersburg PA
CBHW072053110526
44590CB00018B/3149